GOOD FRIENDS

GOOD
FRIENDS

BONDS *that* CHANGE
US *and the* WORLD

PRIYA VULCHI

LEGACY
LIT

New York Boston

Legacy Lit
Hachette Book Group
1290 Avenue of the Americas
New York, NY 10104
LegacyLitBooks.com
@LegacyLitBooks

First edition: April 2025

Legacy Lit is an imprint of Grand Central Publishing. The Legacy Lit name and logo are registered trademarks of Hachette Book Group, Inc.

The publisher is not responsible for websites (or their content) that are not owned by the publisher.

The Hachette Speakers Bureau provides a wide range of authors for speaking events. To find out more, go to hachettespeakersbureau.com or email HachetteSpeakers@hbgusa.com.

Legacy Lit books may be purchased in bulk for business, educational, or promotional use. For information, please contact your local bookseller or the Hachette Book Group Special Markets Department at special.markets@hbgusa.com.

Print book interior by Jeff Stiefel

Library of Congress Cataloging-in-Publication Data

Names: Vulchi, Priya, author.
Title: Good friends : bonds that change us and the world / Priya Vulchi.
Description: First edition. | New York : Legacy Lit, 2025. | Includes bibliographical references.
Identifiers: LCCN 2024046329 | ISBN 9781538766620 (hardcover) | ISBN 9781538766644 (ebook)
Subjects: LCSH: Friendship.
Classification: LCC BF575.F66 V85 2025 | DDC 177/.62—dc23/eng/20241213
LC record available at https://lccn.loc.gov/2024046329

ISBNs: 9781538766620 (hardcover), 9781538766644 (ebook)

Printed in the United States of America

LSC-C

Printing 1, 2025

To my friends.

Good friends make good trouble.

—Kathy Engel, poet, educator, cultural worker,
and a friend of June Jordan's

———————

I live my life in widening circles.

—Rainer Maria Rilke, *The Book of Hours*

Contents

Disclaimer

Some content may be triggering. Chapter 2 includes mention of rape, and in chapter 9, there is mention of suicide. Several names, pronouns, and details have been changed for privacy. Most public-facing friends are referred to by their first names, which is a stylistic choice to help readers see them as friends, not necessarily the icons they have been abstracted into. Some, however, *are* referred to by last names due to explicit requests by them and/or someone close to them I interviewed. Although I distinguish friends from romantic and sexual partners (for clarity's sake), I know these categories can overlap. Additionally, many of the depicted friendships are of artists and activists, because they spoke most directly to me, but you should know, friendships exist vividly in sports, cooking, science, and every other nook and cranny of life, you just have to look for them, which this book will help you do.

Introduction

The Habit of Friendship

IN TENTH GRADE, I met my friend Winona Guo. What happened after felt like Socrates's thought experiment, recorded by Plato in *The Republic* circa 380 BCE:

Socrates asks listeners to imagine being chained alongside others in a cave underground. Your heads are held stationary, so only the wall in front of you is visible. Behind you, a man-made fire burns, and items nearby thrust shadows. You and the others know the world only by its dancing shadows. A plant's shadow *is* a plant. A baby's shadow *is* a baby, and so on.

One day, you alone are unchained, permitted to wander aboveground.

Socrates says, "In the beginning, [you] might only trace the shadows."[1]

Gradually, your eyes adjust. You identify the causality between the sun, a tree, and its shadow. You return to the cave. Except now, plunged into darkness again, you squint desperately. So unaccustomed are you to the dark, you can no longer see any shadows to even begin sharing your discoveries. The others ridicule you.

The allegory invites us to question, what is truth, and what is habit?[2]

You may feel magnetically pulled to your romantic partner, sinking into her oozing warmth. You may feel anchored by your mother, knowing her mind never strays from your well-being. You may feel an unmatched thrill with your siblings, a banter that never slows in roasts. And in this seemingly natural pecking order of things, friends are lackluster: you get busy. You acquire more relationships and obligations with age, so each friend receives less of your time. Friendships become long-distance because of jobs, and visiting is expensive. Plus, along life's journey somehow we get convinced that of all relationships—family, romantic relationships, and professional, to name a few—friendship is the least consequential. Friends are for partying, Sunday brunch, or watching Netflix. They are peripheral, not central bonds. Nobody expects much from friends, so why try to be a good one?

I remember running into an acquaintance named

Claudia. We paused on the corner of Nassau Street, awkward, struggling to catch up, the crosswalk's pixelated red hand flashing. She was an alumna of Princeton University, where I was finishing up undergrad. There was a fallen-from-grace quality that I recognized in her and in others.

Claudia told me she had broken up with her boyfriend. She could not be vulnerable with her guy friends. She did not "actually talk" to any of her social media friends. She was lonely. Community-less. Going through the motions of a corporate job that, she admitted, was actively harming society.

The red hand above the crosswalk turned into a white stick figure. I waved goodbye.

Claudia inserted headphones and walked away.

We have been tracing shadows.

There is something about friendship that could offer an alternate way of living beyond this rote adult lifestyle of loneliness. I knew this personally.

After Eric Garner's murder in 2014, I had advocated for racial literacy with Winona for a decade, fundraising and traveling to all fifty US states to interview strangers about race together, helping racial literacy become a district graduation requirement, running a nonprofit, and authoring racial literacy books with her, too. I could lean against our friendship, trust in its sturdiness, rest in its shade, so I knew friendship was real, even if society directs us away from it.

I decided to dedicate my senior undergraduate research at Princeton to the topic (more about this in the Afterword). With special access to historical archives and world experts in gender, sexuality, and race studies, I researched how the most formidable friends practiced friendship, eventually stumbling upon June Jordan.

June is one of the most published African American writers ever. Despite not being as well-known by the American public, she is well-known by those whose lives she changed through friendship; in San Francisco, after graduating from college, I interviewed her friends, hearing so firsthand.

After reading her prose and poetry, you will hear her in your ear, as I have, guiding your movements toward being more kind, just, and good. June was not a perfect friend, and you are probably not either. I most certainly am not. But her writing proves that our friends are worth fighting for, that it is never too late to be a good friend, and that nobody, no matter your age, no matter your history, is ineligible for friendship.

Many philosophers believed friendship is important. In ancient Rome, Cicero believed it was just as important for human survival as fire and water.³ Conversations about friendship, however, are dominated by men like Cicero, Plato, and Aristotle or made apolitical in pop culture (think of *Bridesmaids*, or *Seinfeld*). Nowhere could I find contributions centering a modern retelling of friendship; how, because there is no wedding ring binding a friend to you, and no familial bond obligating her to you, a good friend is remarkable. How larger forces like nations, gender, sexuality, race, ethnicity, and class all complicate human connection and kindness, and how being a good friend requires intelligence about those differences.

Friendship must be upgraded *even beyond* these ancient models. This is why I weave through ancient philosophers' friendships *and* June Jordan's more contemporary friendships, among others, including the striking friendships of James Baldwin, Toni Morrison, Pat Parker, Audre Lorde, Malcolm X, and Dr. Martin Luther King Jr. I unearth letters, interview noteworthy friends, observe friendship in pop culture, and sprinkle in my own inspired moments in order to dust friendship off for our modern times.

We need a new vocabulary for talking about friendship, and we crave a new template for friendship itself. When friendships are neglected, all the possibilities of friendship—the political possibilities, the possibilities for love, joy, and community—disappear as well.

This book might feel like adjusting to life aboveground, with all its stinging brightness. Unlike Plato's allegory though, the friendships in the following pages will ease your strain, as they have done for me. My hope is that friendship does not just sit more prominently in your head, but that it springs into movement, changing the vibrance and depth of your relationships, improving your ability to connect with your community and even the world. You will learn about how people stay in touch with friends, love friends rigorously, bask in friendship's joyousness, navigate difficult conversations, advocate for one another, and how to cope with friendship heartbreak and betrayal. You will see that, boiled down to its core, friendship is the study of what it means to be human.

Priya,
San Francisco, May 2024

1.

Friendships of Virtue

WINONA IS GENTLE, slow-going, heartfelt, and long-winded; worrisome, sullen, unpretentious, and open-minded. She falls in love quickly, passionately: with a scarf that folds into a hat, a tea flavor, lyric, sentence, street name, and with people. She falls quickly, passionately into tasks too, bumping into cabinets, unresponsive until her name is bellowed. She is a bad listener when focused on something else, but an immaculate one when focused on me.

From Winona, I learned that friendship means weathering frequent changes. Not just personality changes. Friendships change in temperaments ordinarily too, sometimes becoming sullen and unrecognizable. Emerging again like a different season. No friendship is ordinary. Friendships are serendipitous and curious bonds arising under haphazard circumstance, awakening bewilderment that a stranger—someone not biologically or legally fastened to you—can be loved so thunderously even with their seasons; even though after weeks, months, years, you embrace them with fresh eyes all over again. You choose friendship all over again.

Winona's hair was once below her waist, and she vowed to keep it that way, saying it embodied her femininity. Now it is above her earlobe, and she has sharper things to say about femininity and its rules. She is again changing before my eyes, so fast, so uncontrollably, like a city skyscraper appearing overnight. It does not scare me. I once thought friends were reflections of myself, people who, by having similar music or book taste or hobbies, reaffirmed my way of life. From Winona, I learned that a friend is someone who strives to be one.

Aristotle would have said our friendship began incorrectly.

In Raphael's *The School of Athens*, painted in the 1500s, Aristotle stands beside his mentor and friend Plato, caught mid-conversation. His arm stretches, palm toward the earth, like he is gesturing to pause, slow down. In his other hand is a book, its weight supported by a bent leg. His beard is short, but thick, the same golden-mustard color as the hair on his head and the cloth he wears underneath a cornflower-blue fabric. His face turns toward Plato, and Plato, in turn, points one finger toward the sky, beard long and gray, body draped in purple and pink. Behind them, a milky sky with cotton-candy clouds. There is ample light, elucidating Aristotle's rosy rounded cheeks and Plato's silver-gray hairline.

Other depictions of Aristotle are similar: a wide-set jaw, beard cut close to his chin, broad forehead, and wavy dark hair ending at the nape of his bulky neck. Out of all the fiftysomething people Raphael includes in his fresco, Aristotle and Plato's friendship is most principal. Two bodies, cemented in conversation, every other body cascading around them.

In *Nicomachean Ethics*, Aristotle says there are three types of friendship. The first two he calls *friendships of pleasure* and *friendships of utility*.[1]

Friends of pleasure entertain (we party together). Friends of utility are useful (we borrow something from these friends).

My friendship with Winona began as a friendship of utility. In ninth grade, she slipped her fingers through mine upon introduction. I slid my hand free, returning it to my side. Later, she saw me walking down a hallway, music thumping. Winona says I passed her without looking up.

More than a year went by, and a Black man named

Eric Garner was murdered by the New York City Police Department. I was thinking about race. Passing a local bookstore, I noticed the cashier wrapping books through the window; her head was down, her black hair long, and her hands worked in unison, folding glittery sheets over books, whipping scissors through ribbons. Winona. She had tried to hold my hand, I realized, and in a minute or so, as thoughts flowed, one slowed: Winona is Chinese American. I am Indian American. Together, in our predominantly white high school, we are "Asian American."

I thought of her hand in mine. Her grin. They say happiness is the most vaporous thing, but I think Asian American affinity is. I turned from the window, the next thought took the last one's place, and I kept walking.

Sophomore year, I asked Winona to "do something about race with me." Not because I wanted to be friends, but because she seemed curious about race too. She would raise her hand in history class, say something strikingly intelligent about racial formation in the seventeenth century, but quickly, dropping her hand without expanding. There was something there, in her mind, that I wanted to get closer to.

When I was four, a white woman chased my mom, brother, and me into a car—"You dirty pigs!"—as my mom locked the doors, fumbling to dial my dad. I was crying. My mom breathed heavily. Passing the woman later, my mom said nothing; just smiled and gripped my shoulder. Working at a gas station, my dad was called a pig too, although differently—PIG as in "poor Indian grad student"—and he said nothing either. For us, he said, it is about survival. In India, squatting with a mortar and pestle, my great-grandmother would absentmindedly sing, "Happy and glorious, long to reign over us, God save the Queen." There and here, they were colonial subjects. There and here, it was about survival.

But if the first-generation immigrants' lives were about "survival," the second generations' had to be about more.[2] Winona's parents were immigrants too, and on this we agreed.

Hurried, earnest discussions during lunch led to exchanging books, which led to recruiting friends to join us, and then I was on a dark street ringing Winona's doorbell at 3:00 am, because a simple gesture, a hand held on the first day of school, followed by Garner's murder, had set off a cascade of improbable events. Within a year, Winona and I self-published a racial literacy textbook adopted by educators nationwide.

Ours was a friendship of utility. I would sit, researching, moving images on design software to create graphics while Winona napped on the sofa, knees curled to her chin. When my eyelids became heavy, and my coffee cup ringed with brown, I would call Winona's name, glancing at the clock, and she would rise as I took her place. It was tedious, but invigorating. Like running and reaching a distance where your muscles throb and shriek, only to discover that if you keep going, just a bit farther, your body acquiesces, and you reach an ecstasy your brain promised seconds ago was impossible.

When my mom asked who my new friend was, I said, "We are not friends yet. Just professional partners."

I would soon discover Aristotle's third type of friendship: *friendships of virtue*. While friendships of utility and pleasure form because of what you *get* from a friend, friendships of virtue form because of "goodness."

Rather than a transactive, superficial relationship based on pleasure or utility, which is slippery and subject to change with time, friendships of virtue endure because "familiarity has led them to love each other's characters." In other words, friends of virtue love each other's goodness.

And "goodness," Aristotle says, "is an enduring thing."

Goodness can be abstract and subjective. I try defining goodness as the presence or absence of virtues, or qualities commonly understood to be good, like courage, temperance, patience, prudence, wisdom, kindness, humility, and so on. I also try sharpening its meaning through Aristotle's distinction: "Do men love what is good…or what is good for them? These sometime clash."[3]

Both parties, individually, need to be virtuous—or good—according to Aristotle, otherwise friendship disintegrates. Like a building supported by two pillars, if one pillar is flimsy, regardless of the other's strength, the entire edifice will collapse.

My friendship with Winona would have crumbled if we remained friends of utility, bonded by what was good for us individually, not simply by what was good.

"Winona!" I said, spotting her in the hallway after weeks of intense work together. She turned. "Are you okay?"

She nodded, knuckles white around her backpack straps. A crease deepened between her eyebrows.

"Wait, I feel—" Her forehead thudded onto my shoulder. Students rerouted around us in the hallway, like water diverting around a rock.

She was crying, I realized. Crying from exhaustion. Being everywhere and doing everything and being liked by everyone was how she handled Asian American invisibility. Everyone perceived us as monoliths no matter what we did to prove our individuality, so she did it all—just as, back then, my way of coping was with rage.

We looked at each other. And I felt the warmth of recognition. I realized my frustration being Asian American could be looked at differently. As writer Hua Hsu theorizes, Asian American's categorical broadness also makes it "capacious enough" for us both.[4]

Although we started as a friendship of utility, our friendship became a friendship of virtue. I began to admire Winona's character, her virtues—who she is. How she greeted my sharper edges with graciousness, holding my hand even as I pulled away. How she had a knack for nestling into life's more ambiguous emotions without hurry or judgment.

High school came to an end. In our New Jersey school district, racial literacy became a graduation requirement. Winona and I deferred college, hoping to do more. We fundraised enough to travel nationwide and interview over five hundred people about race, and this became the basis for another book and our racial literacy nonprofit. Most memorable was not how the hills rolled and rolled in Troy, Idaho, creating a never-ending horizon, or how in Tahlequah, Oklahoma, the heat swirled and stiffened my tongue, or how in Brattleboro, Vermont, the backyard chickens kept us up all night. Most memorable was our friendship. How thick and fibrous it became.

Before, I had been chugging through the motions, making friendships of utility and pleasure, yet feeling empty and unsure of why. Winona's friendship opened up passage into another reality in which friendship burns dazzlingly. Without friendships of virtue, you might have many friends, but nobody you light up for, nobody who transforms your life's texture and trajectory. Nastasia, in college, was the first person whom I remember leaning my head against, thinking that I would try to love her like I was learning to love Winona. Other good friendships began bursting forth too, like roses unfurling. They were not always new friends, but sometimes old ones who I looked at differently, who I extended an invitation for another kind of friendship to. Although some friendships ended in heartbreak, although my social bandwidth does not always match my intentions, although friendships can be grueling at times, although my friendship with Winona today looks different than ten years ago, after experiencing friendships of virtue, I still cannot settle for anything less in those I call a good friend.

Aristotle says friendship of virtue is the highest form of love.

Today, marriage is the highest form of love. Companionship is romanticized as the purpose of marriage, not friendship. Friends exist only if fun or useful. There are no airport-chasing-goodbye movie scenes for friends, there are barely any songs or literature. With romantic partners, people make vows like, "in sickness or in health," but commitments to friends look like BFF bracelets. Romantic partners are considered soulmates, not friends. Finding romantic partnership is presented as the fundamental quest for meaning and fulfillment, not friendship.

When I was in my first romantic relationship, somebody asked me how my "better half" was doing, and I rambled about Winona until I was interrupted. He had meant my romantic partner, not her.

But what if Winona was my better half, in part because she was not my girlfriend?

Because *at their best*, all relationships resemble friendships of virtue, whether with your lover, parents, or siblings. A relationship inclusive of pleasure and utility, but not limited by it. A sturdier, reciprocal three-dimensional bond unrestricted by short-lived utility or pleasure. If a relationship fails this standard of friendship, we are unobligated to remain embroiled in it. Because despite a relationship's label, such as "parent" or "spouse," at its core, friendship is what it must hope to be.

This changes friendship's entire positioning. It suggests that people are not goods to be picked off shelves by their advantageousness, but that people are people, and what to appreciate is not their profitability, but who they are. Their goodness. If friendship is on the margins of society—a vague, mishandled, and disrespected relationship—Aristotle's friendships of virtue framework tugs it into the center. Friendship is not a secondary, peripheral relationship in our lives. Friendship is the standard. The aspiration.

There is an ecosystem of relationships with varying

degrees of intimacy. In Arabic, there is نديم, a drinking companion and confidant, أنيس, a close friend, جليس, someone who you sit around with, نجي, an intimate friend, and قرين, someone who is like a spiritual double or soulmate (and these are simplified definitions).

Within this ecosystem, friendships of utility and pleasure can exist, but at a balance. Otherwise, you risk conflating friendship as a whole with friendships of utility and pleasure. You risk putting friendship on the back burner, unaware that another type of friendship exists: friendships of virtue. And friendships of virtue in particular, as Aristotle says, can become the strongest and most consequential relationship of your life.

I think about how Winona took the train down from Boston, after we had separated to different colleges, and I drove her to her COVID-19 vaccination appointment in my parents' car, music blasting. We laughed about how the person I was dating thought it was strange to miss class and drive Winona two hours away, waiting another thirty minutes in the car like "some soccer mom, or like she's your wife."

Winona then talked about a friend she had romantic feelings for, and her growing understanding of her queerness. She suggested our friendship was queer too. I asked her why.

Our friendship, she said, rebelled against heteronormative centering of romantic partners. Our friendship, centering each other, was itself queer, a divergent orientation toward relationship-ing that challenges tradition. Being queer, to me, means approaching relationships through a pathway of feeling, as opposed to heteronormative logics like women should only be attracted to men, or that I should love romantic partners more than friends. We had started to introduce each other as "platonic life partners" but during that car ride Winona said, removing her shoes and folding her legs, we should drop the "platonic" because it "only resolves other people's anxieties about whether we have sex or not," as if being committed to a friend is unimaginable absent the sexual.

It was not always unimaginable.

Over two thousand years ago, Aristotle was committed to friendship too. He calls friendship the bond "that seems to hold states together," that enables a "single soul dwelling in two bodies."

A friendship of virtue, Aristotle says, "is one of the most indispensable requirements of life."[5]

2.

The Individual

IN THE 1840s, Henry David Thoreau lived for two years and two months in Walden Pond in Concord, Massachusetts. Thoreau is an American legend. A canonical thinker and writer. He had light pupils and eyelids that curved downward. His hair was ruffled; his beard reached his bow tie. He had a gentle smile. Thoreau's cabin, where he lived at Walden, was engulfed by wilderness. He ate his own vegetables. He sculpted himself, by himself, in the American wilderness.[1]

Individualism is a worldview that champions the individual over the collective. It goes hand in hand with what being an American legend, like Thoreau, is all about: someone self-sufficient, self-made, prosperous through cunningness and hard work alone. Someone able to pull himself up by the bootstraps, grasping at individual glory and success. Like a cowboy traversing the American frontier. Rugged, dauntless, and self-reliant. Like Steve Jobs and Mark Zuckerberg, ruthless men epitomizing the American Dream.

In 1968, writer June Jordan was curious about Thoreau's American Dream. She moved into a little house on the East Coast, beside marsh reeds that rose and reflected perpendicularly across the water. In an essay called, "Waking Up in the Middle of Some American Dreams," she describes how hawks would sweep low, wings beating "inches from [her] face." Spiders spun their webs, and she could hear them.[2] Come nighttime, she tossed with fear. What was that? The crunch of a twig in otherwise chilling silence. A deep darkness, like a pit, curtained her bedroom's glass walls. During the day, the skies had its moods, changing theatrically within minutes. She had no pets. She disregarded her phone. A poet and activist, she was experimenting with individualism. Locked away from performance or social activity within that rugged American wilderness. Refusing external clamor in order to safeguard a silence that supposedly chiseled legends.

One of those legends was her neighbor, a famous painter. He labored on his canvas seven days a week. June approached him once, wondering why he worked so hard all by himself.

He shrugged. "What else is there to do?"

June processed "his response as ultimate proof of his wisdom and of his genius as a human being: He lived alone. He worked all of the time. He was famous. He was rich. Nobody disturbed him. Nobody lived close enough to try." In her writings, she never mentions his name, just says that by American standards he was "indisputably successful." She imagined herself in his company, distinguishing herself too within a "pseudo-Walden Pond," like Henry David Thoreau.

June was a formidable activist, writer, and friend. I first saw her, leaning against a wall with her arms behind her back, in a documentary about her good friend writer Toni Morrison. In the film, June goes on television and advocates for Toni's work to be recognized by international literary establishments (after which Toni becomes a Nobel Laureate), but then June vanishes.[3] Her name appears again and again alongside Audre Lorde, Angela Davis, and other influential figures of the time, but always too quickly. As I approached her work, it seemed June was always turning the corner.

I finally picked up her book, *Some of Us Did Not Die*, featuring a selection of her essays. Who was this person repeatedly called not only a great activist but also a remarkable friend?

In *Some of Us Did Not Die*, June writes about her time inside that isolated cottage, marinating within the American Dream: imagine treks through crisp autumnal cold, and steaming coffee inside porcelain mugs.

But trouble arrived quickly.

"Truly traditional/deranged/American images of the good life kept me in that wilderness, that willful loneliness, until somebody else came into the little house and raped me."

Screaming seemed futile, June writes about the rape. She thought about her neighbor, the painter. She thought about their situation: she was assaulted, and he was suffering from suicidal ideation—as she had gradually learned—despite his fame and wealth. After being assaulted, she needed his help, but she never asked. Maybe he needed her, but he never asked. Both were ensnared by myths of American individualism; individualism is about self-interest and isolating yourself to guard self-interest. Individualism is when the parameters of care hug tightly only around you.

Every "American one of us," as June writes, is raised to believe in our individual specialness, a specialness that makes every problem especially yours, and especially not mine. Her neighbor, mere meters away, had forsworn all company. He would not help her, June felt sure of, because he would not care.

"What does it mean to be a legend to all," June wonders in her essay, "and a friend to none?"

Unbeknownst to June was that Thoreau, whose individualist lifestyle she attempted to mimic, actually built his cabin on a friend's land, writer and abolitionist Ralph Waldo Emerson. On any given day, their silhouettes could be spotted strolling around Walden Pond, heads down, deep in dialogue.[4] Thoreau was never alone, as June and the rest of us have presumed. Rather than being emblematic of American individualism, Thoreau is actually emblematic of friendship, and how it challenges individualism.

Not all friendships, though. Friendships of utility and pleasure only bolster individualism. They give it legs. These friendships detain care within the parameters of self: I either get something useful from you, or you provide me with pleasure. By practicing centering yourself in these friendships, always wondering how these friendships can benefit you, you become fluent in individualism's language.

Friendships of utility and pleasure not only make you well-versed in individualism, they also make you literally alone. Individuals. Because they snap quickly. They are weaker relationships, which may be fun or useful at times, but do not endure, because they are not strong. They are unable to withstand changing circumstances and inevitable hard times, so they flutter away easily, especially with age.

"For if the one party is no longer pleasant or useful," Aristotle says, "the other ceases to love him."[5]

In one magazine comic, a friend says to another friend, "Great seeing you!! If you're ever in New York, in my neighborhood, and on my block, let's get together!"[6]

Maybe their friendship lived primarily on social media, and offline they were less fun. Maybe they partied together, and as they became less interested in partying, their common denominator dwindled, so their friendship dwindled too.

Generation Z is crowned the loneliest generation. Twenty-three percent of adults under twenty-five suffer from "loneliness and workplace isolation," which has similar health effects to smoking fifteen cigarettes a day.[7] Loneliness escalates because our social bonds are frail. Because they are predominantly friendships of pleasure and utility. And when our friendships are frail, we lose them. We become more and more atomized. More and more alone.

Friendships of virtue, however, intervene.

We are hurtling toward individualism, but friendships of virtue slow the fall.

Aristotle says friendships of virtue are made of friends "who are good, and alike in virtue; for these wish well alike to each other...and they are good themselves."[8]

Instead of approaching friendships like a transaction,

calculating personal gains or what is extractable, therefore continuing to narrow your self-interest, friendships of virtue enlarge your self-interest to include a friend's well-being too. American individualism does not guide us in this direction. It teaches us to tighten our self-interests, squeezing our friendships out.

In 1976, Steve Jobs and Steve Wozniak started Apple in a garage. In photos, they lean over computers, beaming side by side. Then, Wozniak says in an interview, "He changed his personality forever because he now was a founder of a company that had money. He wanted so strongly to find the way to be an important person in the world."[9]

In the film *Steve Jobs*, Wozniak approaches Jobs, hurt by Jobs's fame and his own lack of recognition.[10] Jobs wears a suit and tie, his hair slicked back. He listens to Wozniak, impatient, then says, "I play the orchestra. And you're a good musician."

By deleting Wozniak from the narrative, minimizing his contributions, Jobs's character confirms to audiences that individualism is the cost of genius.

"[The] idea that as an individual, you're going to work hard, and you're going to make it on your own—'invisibilizes' all of the help that people do get," says community curator Mia Birdsong on the podcast, *How to Talk to People*.[11]

The distorted lore about Jobs and Thoreau obsesses over their self-reliance. Yet, Jobs had Wozniak and Thoreau had Emerson; in fact, Thoreau's mom frequently visited to do his laundry.[12]

Modern American culture calls us to greatness, implores us to become someone great. A great parent and spouse. A great mathematician, scientist, or artist, even a recipient of a Nobel, Grammy, or Time's Person of the Year. As a child, few aspire primarily to be a great friend. Yet, the trick to being great is to be good first. Good friendship enables greatness.

Through extensive propaganda, however, American individualism insists that friends are not worth the trouble. It informs us that the furthest our self-interests can expand, albeit shakingly, is around a romantic partner and nuclear family—maximum.

With my romantic partner, I notice how we are pinned in iMessages. He texts me good night, and me good morning. If I ever feel worthless, I snuggle into this assurance of worth. His incessant attention. We both deliver on our ends of a delusion, that we are special, that we are each other's, and that each other is all we need.

Meanwhile, I neglect my friends, because of all relationships, friendships seem the least consequential, or the most forgiving. Life increasingly becomes about protecting your own self-interest. Friendships creep onto the back burner. Individualism expands, its teeth in friendship like a bulldog with meat. As students, we are immersed in friendships, in walkable communities like a college campus, with friends only a knock away. As adults, we turn more and more inward toward a romantic partner and nuclear family. We do not share healthcare with friends, only a spouse. We do not get tax breaks from friends, only a spouse. In dorm rooms, there are photos of friends; in homes, none.

What friendships of virtue do, however, is stretch our imaginations. What if we committed ourselves to friends like we commit ourselves to people legally and biologically tied to us? What if my self-interest did not just include me, or my nuclear family, but also someone who is extralegal and unrelated—a once-stranger? What if whatever happens to them, implicates me too?

My mom's childhood friend, Auntie B, is a single mother. This month, Auntie B drove alone from Nevada to Texas to live near her daughter, her life loaded into a van.

My mom looked at my dad, "If you were driving from Nevada to Texas, I would have come with you." She looked sad. "I thought I should go with her. I kept thinking I should go with her. I am not sure why I could not do that for my friend."

If they had a friendship of virtue, the friends in that

magazine comic would meet, even if never coincidentally in the same city, in the same neighborhood, or on the same block. Jobs would not have erased Wozniak. My mom would have accompanied Auntie B.

Friends of virtue offer a refuge when you need to gather your thoughts, as Emerson did for Thoreau. They check in on you, inviting you to dine with their family, as Emerson did for Thoreau. They care for you during illness, as June's friends did while she fought breast cancer: June shares how Adrienne arrived from Santa Cruz to share poetry, laughter, and lunch; how Angela drove her to the doctor; Lauren brought her food; Stephanie organized her friends into a digital network; Phyllis cared for the garden; Sara helped her give blood; Camille brought medicine at midnight; Pratibha traveled from London to visit; and Martha from New York.[13]

Friendships of virtue are where individualism fades, where your self-interests turn porous. Friendships, June writes, is a "love that supersedes given boundaries of birthright or birthplace or conventions of romance or traditions of loyalty. It is love that yields to no boundary. It is one love that takes you to its bosom and that saves your life."[14]

Good friendship disrupts individualism. Like a baker pulling dough, friendships of virtue stretch your self-interest to include a friend too.

I remember as our college graduations approached, Winona FaceTimed me from her dorm in Boston. She was making tea, and, releasing a tea bag into a mug, said that someone had asked her about her postgraduation plans.

"What did you say?"

"That I would be with you," she said with gentle finality. A grin.

My cheeks did not flush in surprise, my head did not spin. We never discussed it before, but I knew.

I thought about June, sitting alone in the wilderness, after her assault, listening to the ticking of her kitchen clock, and the humming of her refrigerator.

June decided to move back to the city. Back to where there was noise, people, less theory, and more "direct contact, direct conflict," and the "actual touch of tenderness." She did not want privacy and fame, like her neighbor the painter, she wanted public transportation and crowded restaurants. She did not want to be a legend. She wanted her friends. She wanted to "exhume earlier systems of extended kinship," and apply it to the twenty-first century.

American individualism is a dead end. Friendships of virtue are a way out.

"Misbegotten American dreams," June writes, "have maimed us all."[15]

3.

Politics of Friendship

ONCE UPON A time, friendships were epic, heroic, and political relationships. The motto "liberté, égalité, fraternité" from the French Revolution, for instance, is engraved all over French buildings.[1] "Fraternité" looks like men thrusting flags into the air, representing a politically grandiose friendship. In ancient Greece, the word "hetairos" was common too, meaning a companion or comrade, as scholar Patricia Vesely explains. Hetairos sharpens how we imagine friendships by giving friendship a political bend. Suddenly, friendship has tremendous political power. In fact by the fifth century BCE, "*hetairos* were associations that often held specific political goals and were influential in shaping Athenian democracy."[2]

Today, we envision friendships as polite, demure, and

apolitical relationships, like the television show *Friends*. You get coffee with a friend; you do not go to war with them, do not start revolutions with them. Political alliances are framed as cold, distanced bonds and friendships as warm, cozy ones. Political bonds look like soldiers propped on elbows inside a trench, their unanimity emphasized, and their individuality squashed. If asked what the soldier's name next to you was, although you would die for him, you might not know.[3] Our friendships are different: they are sweet and intimate.

But our friendships are still political. You might not be wielding swords, but your friendships are no less disruptive. Every interaction you have with a friend is pregnant with possibility, a moment of political significance, whether you know it or not.

We see the world in two buckets, "the political," which includes race, gender, class, sexuality, among other political forces, and "the personal," or everything we imagine as apolitical, things like real estate, skiing, and friendships. But the more you think about it, the more difficult it becomes to distinguish the personal from the political. There is real estate, but there is gentrification and racial redlining, too. You invite your friends on a ski trip, but consider how expensive the sport is, and what are the class components of that? Political forces pulse through even seemingly private matters. As feminist Carol Hanisch said, the personal *is* political.

When two friends meet, their intersecting identities—whether nationality, gender, or class—create opportunities *and* obstacles for connection.

In the early sixties, June Jordan read an article by social scientist and activist Frances Fox Piven. She wrote Frances an angry letter, challenging her opinion, and Frances wrote back—she wanted June to come over and talk.[4]

In her essay, "Civil Wars," June writes, "We did not change each other's minds but we did come to respect the sincerity of our differences. And then we became close friends."

Frances was white and lived in Harlem with her daughter, who was nearly the same age as June's son.

"Each of us was raising one child and also pursuing a complicated professional and political life," June says. "You could accurately describe Frances as a brilliant and radical humanitarian; her commitment to poor people and to Black people cannot, anywhere, be easily matched. But there are things that we never talk about, or never talk about, twice."

One day, June and Frances arrived for lunch in New York City. June asked Frances about a pending California referendum that sought to fire any educator who was "publicly homosexual."

Frances said, "Oh, gay rights."

June said no, civil rights.

Frances believed June's "loving a woman" was whimsical "deviant behavior" that distracted from other humanitarian issues, more serious things. June disagreed sharply. Other unspoken hurts, on Frances's end, began crawling out too.

June writes, "I remember thinking that the cafe table where we sat was really as large as the whole country and that now we had taken irreconcilable, opposite sides."

"It seemed to me that my silence on these issues and my continuing self-denial around the 'issue' of my bisexuality was what had kept the friendship alive. Without my collaboration, without my self-censorship, the disagreements between us seemed irreconcilable."[5]

After that lunch, June and Frances stopped talking.

"The bond of friendship exposes the friends to each other," writes Grand Valley State University Professor Darren Walhof. "While we might be able to maintain a projected image of ourselves in our professional relations or in our encounters with strangers, we denote others as friends precisely because it is with them that such projections fade away and our 'true' selves are more exposed."[6]

If friendship exposes people to one another, what do our true selves feel, look, and sound like? Are they sanitized beings, untouched by politics? Or is your true self actually shaped deeply by political forces and politicized realities, whether your race, gender, sexuality, class, nationality, or ability?

If we tiptoe around "the political," we tiptoe around friends, too. We never get to know friends, beyond superficial interactions. Friends cannot cling onto similarities, scared to meander where those similarities end. Evading the political keeps friendship tangential, without the chance to depart from peripheral relationships into central and deeply loving ones. Evasion keeps friendship "easy," and, thus, shallow. Evasion means insisting life occurs in a void, apart from forces like white supremacy, patriarchy, and capitalism. We fragment the personal realm of our lives from its political contexts, disregarding how the personal has everything to do with the political. Pretending otherwise just permits friends to suffer from political inequity while we feign innocence.

June tried quieting her bisexuality to stay friends with Frances. You cannot, however, sever a limb and expect your body to not bleed out.

June writes, "The answer is that suicide is absolute, and if you think you will survive by hiding who you really are, you are sadly misled: There is no such thing as partial or intermittent suicide. You can only survive if you—who you really are—do survive."[7]

Who you are is inherently political. How people perceive and treat you based on your accent, skin color, eye
shape, citizenship, who you love, where you grew up, what
school you went to, the amount of money in your wallet,
how you perceive and treat people too, all that matters.
Friendship means you are, uncoerced by law or biology,
unafraid to claw past layers of political barriers, calcified
by generations to reach a friend, to be a good friend. World
War II internment camps kept Japanese American youth
from friendships outside the camps. Jim Crow racial seg-
regation kept Black children from befriending white children, among others. And today, these barriers' remnants
and the novel ways they have evolved to continue thriving,
including through our pedagogy, media, and culture, still
keep friends apart, slipping into our minds, if not literally
between our bodies. This is how friendship is political.
Friendship persists not without political differences but
because of them. Every moment of friendship is its own
political battle.

When it comes to friendship, Aristotle was a conserva-
tive thinker, not a revolutionary one. He preferred keeping
political engagement out of friendship. He conceptualizes
hetairos, the word conveying political friendship, as separate from friendships of virtue.[8] Aristotle avoids the politicalness of friendship, because he believed friendship was

suitable for elite men alone. He believed women could not be friends with one another or with men, because they were inferior. There was no need to discuss political differences, because there were few differences in his friendships to begin with.[9]

Scholar Ivy Schweitzer writes about Aristotle's friendships of virtue, "The word 'virtue,' one of the defining requirements for ideal friendship, captures this gender specificity, since its Latin root *vir* translates as 'man.'"[10]

So much of our modern understanding of friendship has not progressed from Aristotle's thinking. We cannot learn friendship from someone who did not see you—you, as a non-elite member of society, for whatever reason that may be—as worthy of friendship in the first place. Friendship will fall flat on its face, like it has today, if we continue with Aristotle's blueprint. We will keep it small and to the side, not knowing what else to do with it. Like Emerson and Thoreau, you might give friends physical safety. Like June and her friends, you might nurture friends during sickness, but it will still be inadequate. Love will still require something else. Your friendships might feed you, but they will never satiate. If we attempt friendship like Aristotle, excluding and mishandling friends' political identities, we cannot be good friends.

To fill the gap that Aristotle left, we can turn to others.

Black feminists like June Jordan push our thinking, refashioning friendship to include us all.

Difference does not have to settle into hierarchy. Friendship, which aspires for mutuality, reciprocity, and equity amid differences, is an act of political resistance. Good friends do not see the political as separate from the personal, like oil separated from water, but as a route to achieving *even more* personal intimacy with friends.

In 2019, the BBC listed *Giovanni's Room* as one of the hundred most influential novels ever in 2019. At first, however, it was highly scrutinized. His US publisher, Knopf, wanted James to keep writing about Black life in Harlem, like in his previous popular book *Go Tell It on the Mountain. Giovanni's Room* was too niche, too controversial. It had white main characters; not only that, they were queer.

His publisher said, "You cannot afford to alienate [your] audience. This new book will ruin your career, because you're not writing about the same things and in the same manner as you were before, and we won't publish this book as a favor to you."[11]

Despite this, in 1958, *Giovanni's Room* was being revised for stage production. So when James sat dully in a theater studio one winter, listening to people critique *Giovanni's Room*, likely for being too queer, he was used to it. By censoring *Giovanni's Room*, people were censoring

James too, preferring his queerness silenced, preferring he stuck to what sold well: his Blackness. What took James by surprise was when a young Black woman, "a small, shy, determined person," as James describes her, began defending him from all the way up in the workshop bleachers.

She started "taking on some of the biggest names in the American theater because she had liked the play and they, in the main, hadn't," James writes. "I was enormously grateful to her, she seemed to speak for me; and afterward she talked to me with a gentleness and generosity never to be forgotten."[12]

It was Lorraine Hansberry. James knew of her—twenty-nine years old, just a few years younger than him, a playwright, writer, and organizer—but did not know her. Lorraine, with her signature short hair, cropped right above her earlobes, and round inquisitive eyes, began defending *Giovanni's Room*, perhaps knowing that it was critical for theater audiences: queerness and race had to be confronted together. James could not bifurcate his queerness from his race, just like you cannot surrender your head from your body.

James and Lorraine eventually became close friends.

Really loving your friends, so that your self-interest includes them too, necessitates political engagement; it is a day-to-day involvement with your friends' well-being *that* deep. Lorraine could not love James fully without loving *him* fully, his queerness, Blackness, and everything in between and beyond.

Paraphrasing the French philosopher Jacques Derrida, the writer Hua Hsu said that friendship's intimacy is in the "sensation of recognizing oneself in the eyes of another."[13] To see you fully, to recognize herself in you, friends need to see your complete world, so that you can speak freely, laugh and cry together, so that it could be a relationship of depth. Friends cannot arrive at your friendship veiled by apolitical-ness, asking you to cleave an important part of yourself in order to become more palatable or easy for them. You are either loved fully, or not loved at all. Good friendship is a politically aware friendship. If friends are metaphorically oceans apart—coming together from different nationalities, languages, races, gender identities, and more—we should be intelligent about navigating those oceans, conscious of their currents, where their intertidal zones are, in order to cross them and reach one another safely. We cannot pretend ignorance and hope to stay afloat.

Lorraine wrote the first Broadway play penned by a Black woman, *A Raisin in the Sun.* She received lots of criticism, in addition to fame.

When she was attacked publicly once, James called her, "and all [Lorraine] said—with a wry laugh—was, 'My

God, Jimmy, do you realize you're only the second person who's called me today? And you know how my phone kept ringing before!'"[14]

Lorraine loved James even when it was difficult, and James loved Lorraine back with the same ferocity. Whether bridging barriers between queerness and heteronormativity, between fame and unjust public scrutiny, good friendship refuses shutting your eyes and covering your ears when things get "political." Good friendship is brave, it greets the politicalness of our lives too, seeing it as inseparable from who we are. Political consciousness does not detract from good friendship but deepens it.

The personal is political. If we neglect how political systems sculpt our daily moods, relationships, successes, and failures, loving each other becomes impossible. Inches between us gape as wide as the whole country.

Embracing the political in friendship does not mean seeing friends as caricatures, as their race, gender, and nothing else; it means granting friends the three-dimensionality we grant even book characters. Friends are in dynamic relationships with their race, gender, and other political forces, but they are so much more, too.

Poet and activist Pat Parker explained it neatly in her poem called "For the white person who wants to know how to be my friend." She writes, "The first thing you do is to forget that i'm Black. Second, you must never forget that i'm Black."[15]

Friendship is political, because in a world where no friend is equal to another, good friendship mandates political awareness. Also, because friendship *itself*—simply attempting friendship—is already a political act. Being a good friend feels like swimming against the current, because you are. Friendship is unsupported by society because it is dangerous to it. Capitalism prefers people individualistic and uncaring. Society is structured so that we become more and more alone, and thus, more and more selfish and profit oriented. You get tunnel vision, becoming highly self-interested. Life becomes about "me, me, me:" my career, my family, my job, and my nation. Friendship, however, expands your purview, shaking things up, turning "me" toward "you" and gradually toward "us."

Loving friends in a world that claws and tears them down, convincing us to bare our teeth, is itself a political feat. You might not know it, but every time you are a good friend, even though you are tired, even though it is hard, is its own moment of political defiance.

In the past, people would ask friends for favors regularly, including rides to the airport, for some sugar, or to borrow a dress. Over time, in our increasingly capitalistic society, asking has started to feel impolite, since we *could* do it independently. Content creator Amelia Montooth explains how, instead of asking for a ride to the airport, you could order an Uber. Instead of borrowing sugar, you could use Postmates. Rather than borrowing a dress, you could order one on Amazon.

"It drives us further into isolation from each other and from our friends," Montooth says. "Which is good for literally no one except for the people who are trying to sell us stuff on our phones."[16]

After simple requests, we text friends "no worries if not!!" but asking friends for favors should be normalized. Friends should not be inconveniences. Friendship's small-favor economy creates opportunities to spend more time with friends, deepen relationships, and simultaneously challenges capitalist overconsumption and unrealistic pressures to be self-reliant.

Friendship is lasting affection for people beyond your self-interest. It is a real love beyond capitalist and individualistic scripts. You might not think driving your friend to the airport is political, but it is.

Politically loving friendships do not have to be so rare; they were not always. The very meaning of a friend implicates the political. In English, "friend" comes from the Old English word "freon," meaning, "to love, like, honor, set free (from slavery or confinement)."[17]

When you do experience good friendship, it sears you with love that you experience at your core. In feeling better understood, you feel better loved, too. Friendship becomes an "ongoing activity," never a dull moment, because although you can never fully understand each other, you remain resolved to keep trying.[18] You do not tolerate political differences, good friendship obliges you to love your way through them. And if friends survive this dynamism— never condescendingly presuming absolute knowledge of each other, remaining attentive and curious, always open to a friend's many-splendored-ness, including their inherent politicalness—it indicates a respect for friends' full, unrestricted humanity.

We love watching the television show *Friends*, but we are perplexed why our friendships fail to live up to its image. *Friends* only works in fiction: an all-white cast sipping coffee, the world beyond never penetrating their insulated bubble. In real life, people cannot sit idly side by side, never interacting with political forces weaving between them. Even if your friends share one identity, like race as in *Friends*, your nationality, ability, ethnicity, sexuality, and class remain at play.

For friendships to rise, roaring, branching up and out, exploding with colorful possibilities, becoming what it once was—"the essential harmonic quality of the cosmic sphere," as the pre-Socratic philosopher Pythagoras believed—then we must embrace it for what it is: inherently political.[19] The more you lean into friendship's politicalness, the more you lean into good friendship.

Political friendship is not soldiers fighting on a battlefield, or news anchors debating one another on television. Rather, it is tender; it is when friends look at you and ask you to love them for who they are.

As June writes, "The moral and political measurement of a life will not be taken only according to legislative outcome of a campaign, or battlefield body counts after the battle." Instead, the "moral measurement of a life will also happen hour by hour, and according to every single interpersonal episode."[20]

Treating "every single interpersonal episode" of friendship with integrity demands political awareness. You cannot cleave the political from the personal. None of us are genderless, raceless, or classless amorphous bodies floating through a raceless, genderless, or classless world. We are, and we live in, the exact opposite.

Politicalness is not irrelevant to friendship, it is principle.

Love is intrinsically a political task.

4.

Friends Make
the World Better

WHEN JUNE JORDAN met her friend, activist-scholar Angela Davis, Angela already had an international reputation. In 1970, FBI director J. Edgar Hoover put her on the FBI's Ten Most Wanted Fugitives List. She was twenty-six years old, with a PhD from Berlin, and an assistant professor at University of California Los Angeles. Falsely accused and charged of murder, she was captured and jailed. Thousands countrywide organized for her freedom. Yoko Ono and John Lennon penned a song called "Angela." Her face was plastered on posters and pins. In 1972, after sixteen months, she was released and acquitted as not guilty.[1]

Angela called June first to arrange a meeting, maybe curious about June's work. When June answered the phone,

Angela thought she was a child. Not because June's voice lacked "maturity," but because June spoke so earnestly, like she was offering you "everything she had."[2]

They became good friends. In one photo from the documentary *A Place of Rage*, they complement each other: Angela has long hair, June has short hair; Angela wears big hoops dangling from her ears, June wears small ones; Angela has on a gray top over black pants, and June, a black top over a gray skirt. Their bodies lean toward each other, like magnets. Their smiles are not posed, but leak out of them, like two kids in the middle of a good laugh, fighting for air before a teacher catches them.[3]

Sometime during their friendship, June's doctor recommended she see an oncologist. Adrienne Torf, June's primary partner, accompanied her. Once there, however, the oncological surgeon dismissed June, saying a biopsy was unnecessary.

Adrienne objected, "But what if the biopsy could turn out positive?"

June woke up under the general anesthesia's fog.

Another doctor looked down at her. He held her shoulders. He held her steady.

"We found cancer. It's cancer. You have breast cancer," he said.

After her mastectomy, June had trouble looking at her

chest, which had to be dressed daily with bandages to blanket her wound. Adrienne was by her side, but she wondered, "who among my devoted friends could really tolerate" her condition.[4] Sometimes, the hardest part of friendship is feeling deserving of friendship.

It was Angela, however, who had joined Adrienne and June at the hospital for June's mastectomy. "It was Angela," June writes, "who read everything published on breast cancer and who drove me to the doctor on the morning when the doctor told me that the cancer had spread to the lymph nodes and that, consequently, he was revising his prognosis from 80 percent likely to survive to 40 percent."

It was Angela who then drove June to a neighborhood salon, the new prognosis ringing in their ears, begging the hairdresser "to do something." The hairdresser dyed an "electric orange" stripe of hair across June's head.[5]

Good friends have this kind of steadfastness, in good times or in bad. You cannot turn friendship on and off. You are either a friend or you are not. You are either there for friends in times of need, or not. Friends might think they do not matter, and the world often conspires to confirm that they do not. Good friends demand that they do. They demand action. Most people would not abandon a friend when sick. But what most friends do not understand is that, in the same way an illness or personal failure knocks you down, political injustices do too. Diseases do not just make people sick, injustice does too.

Aristotle said that for a friendship to be good, each friend must "wish well alike to each other"; meaning, each friend wishes for the other's well-being.[6] But friendship cries out for more than superficial well-wishes. Could I be a friend, committed to a friend's well-being only by wishing her well? Friendship necessitates more. It requires fighting the systems that directly interfere with a friend's wellness. Friends that do not demonstrate care for your freedom are not friends, they are acquaintances. This can feel bleak, dismal—we might realize that we cannot call many people good friends. This is all right. Our bars *should* be raised. Not every uncategorizable relationship is friendship. We need a standard for who we call a good friend.

June says, "It is not only who you are…but what we can do for each other that will determine the connection."[7]

Angela and June fought for each other during both personal and political troubles, seeing them as indistinguishable. In a piece Angela published after June's death in 2002, she remembers June's laugh, a high-pitched giggle. The two women were fierce advocates, and through the heaviness of their work, whether Angela's fighting for the abolition of the prison-industrial complex, or June's advocacy against the war on Afghanistan, Angela would call June "sometimes for no other reason than to feel the exhilaration of her protracted laughter."

Angela credited June for stirring in her and others, a sense of "their own responsibility to make the world better."[8]

Friends make this link for each other, from an okay world to a better one. The steadfastness that friends demonstrate—Angela, reading everything on breast cancer, driving June to and from appointments—is why friendship has been one of the greatest forms of political action. Activism is not usually associated with friendship, but the best friendships consist of it.

Traditional ideas of activism create thresholds that ordinary people feel they do not meet. In reality, people were never aware they were making history. The Black activists we admire got up and had to figure out how to ride the bus, how to attend school. We think social change is accreditable to heroes. Icons. Someone elite or extraordinary, distinguished from regular people with some prescriptive plan. But our world was transformed by ordinary friends, not icons. Political action does not, and has never, looked like what we learn as textbook activism.

Political action cannot mean showing up to a protest,

then going home, never to think about it again. While pro-testing and marching are necessary, most issues today do not lack awareness but devotion and creativity toward how that action is. They lack the thousands of nonobvious acts by nonobvious people.

On January 24, 1988, Americans everywhere from California to Texas to Delaware bent down to retrieve the *New York Times*. Inside, above the centerfold was a black-and-white photograph of Toni Morrison. The headline in thick black ink said, "Black Writers in Praise of Toni Morrison," with forty-eight Black writers' signatures underneath.[9]

A month earlier, June was having an ordinary lunch with Toni, her friend and renowned novelist. Conversation veered into how Toni had not yet received a national prize, not the National Book, National Book Critics Circle awards, or the Pulitzer Prize.

On one hand, who cared about such prizes? They fixated on white respectability politics, literature written for white people, which Toni's books were uninterested in.

In *Toni Morrison: The Pieces I Am*, Toni talks about "the little white man that sits on your shoulder and checks out everything you do or say," and how she tries getting rid of him while writing.

"You sort of knock him off and, you know, you're free."[10]

On the other hand, recognition matters. Just a month

before June's lunch with Toni, James Baldwin had died without winning a keystone literary prize, despite his success. Looking at Toni, another Black artist being overlooked, June saw her friend's confidence thinning. Toni was devastated. Picking up her pen in the mornings, Toni had been feeling discouraged.

June and another friend, scholar Houston A. Baker Jr., wrote both the letter and statement that appeared in the *New York Times*, gathering forty-six other prominent signatures along with them.

"Despite the international stature of Toni Morrison, she has yet to receive the national recognition that her five major works of fiction entirely deserve," the statement read. "We write this testament of thanks to you, dear Toni: alive, beloved and persevering, magical."

Toni was stunned. "This is for me?" she asked.

"You bet. You bet," June said over the phone. "Who else?"[11]

Toni won the Pulitzer Prize for fiction that same year.

Cosmetic fixes do not fix an underlying disease. Surface-level actions do not make dents. A commitment to a friend, however, can.

In Little Rock, Arkansas, Winona and I met civil rights activist Dr. Sybil Jordan Hampton after interviewing students in Little Rock Central High School—a location canonized in our textbooks by the infamous 1957 photograph of Elizabeth Eckford, a Black girl walking to class while white women, foaming at the mouth, stalk her up to the entrance, protesting her and the other eight Black students (the "Little Rock Nine") for desegregating Central High. The current Central High students' stories were not unfamiliar: the I-630 highway racially divided the town, classes were still racially divided, and while the school is no longer segregated, it is not integrated either.

Sharing this with Sybil over dinner, I chewed fish, warm bread between my fingers, the candlelight deepening the pensive crease between Sybil's brows and reflecting off her golden earrings. In school, out of a class of 544 people, Sybil was the only Black student. Not once, for years, did anyone speak to her. She finally graduated as the first Black student to attend Central High from tenth to twelfth grade, following in the Little Rock Nine's footsteps, yet she is largely unknown compared to the Little Rock Nine.

Sybil's knife clicked against the plate as she cut some vegetables. She said, "You don't see that there are a thousand or thousands of unnamed people who were engaged in the struggle, who made sacrifices, who put one brick on a road that took a billion bricks. We are a culture that loves icons and heroes. When so many young people ask the question, 'What can I do? I can't be like the Little Rock

Nine!' It's because we created this sense that that's what it takes to create change."

I remember speaking to Butler Browder in Montgomery, Alabama, whose mother, Aurelia Browder, was one of four plaintiffs in a 1956 Supreme Court case that desegregated US buses. Seven months before Rosa Parks's historic arrest, Aurelia was forced from her bus seat for a white man and woman; Mary Louise Smith, Claudette Colvin, and Susie McDonald, the other plaintiffs, experienced similar discrimination.

Butler said in one interview, "Five women had stories to tell: instances of individual mistreatment. They came together to change things for the world. Their concern at the time was not for their own personal thoughts or beliefs, but the beliefs and the theories of a whole."[12]

Sitting with him in his childhood home, Butler told Winona and me that he was worried for our generation, because we did not know the real history. It was not any icon, he said, but a group of Black women, *friends*, who changed things—he knew so firsthand, watching his mother as a boy. I glanced at his white T-shirt, his mother and her friends' photographs pasted onto it, with the text "World's Most Courageous Women" arching like a rainbow. I saw how that boy turned into a man fighting for their story, in a world where Rosa Parks alone reigned in American history books instead.

Our reality has been wrung out of shape. Our world's greatest architects are friends, not individuals. Justice seems like a lofty goal, but friendship brings it back to earth. Friendship becomes a place to start, and a reason to keep going. We do not need to wake up aspiring to change the world through one heroic outsized action. Change unfolds from the everyday acts of caring for people fiercely, one by one, through the incentivizing and pressing bonds of friendship.

You might think, of course these Black friends had politically active friendships. Fighting for one another meant fighting for their own wellness, too—not just a friend's. Angela and June's political friendship makes sense, because their oppressions overlapped as two Black women in America. But June took action even for friends unlike her, even when it was unbeneficial. Even when the cost was high.

Motivation for political action, especially for people unlike us, does not descend into our hearts unprovoked. Friendship sets it aflame; it is the spark for any successful movement. It connects people we never imagined sharing a meal with, bridging differences in nationality, age, class, ability, race, sexuality, and gender.

Malcolm X and Yuri Kochiyama met in 1963. A popular photograph of Yuri captures her on the streets, speaking into a megaphone's detachable microphone wearing sharp cat-eyed glasses, hair knotted under a bandanna, determination etched into her brow.[13] Yuri's parents were Japanese immigrants, issei. In the 1940s, Yuri and the rest of her family were forced into horse stalls in Santa Anita, California, and later into a concentration camp in Jerome, Arkansas, for two years. When Yuri met Malcolm over two decades later, she was the mother of six children and living in a Harlem housing project. She approached Malcolm at a protest, challenging one of his political stances. Their conversation afterward resulted in a lifelong friendship.

Yuri said, "He certainly changed my life. I was heading in one direction, integration, and he was going in another, total liberation, and he opened my eyes."[14]

Traveling through Africa and the Middle East, Malcolm mailed postcards to Yuri. Once returned, he went to Yuri's apartment, where Yuri arranged for him to meet Hiroshima and Nagasaki atomic bomb survivors. The kitchen, hallway, and every bedroom were filled with mostly local Black, white, and Puerto Rican civil rights activists. None of them were "Malcolm's people—no nationalists, no Muslims, no radicals."

Malcolm listened to the atomic bomb survivors through a translator.

"He knew about Asian history so well. We couldn't believe it," Yuri said.

The next year, Malcolm was onstage in New York, and a commotion broke out in the audience. Yuri turned to look.

Suddenly, gunfire.

Snapping her head back, Yuri saw Malcolm fall backward. Chaos erupted, people ducked and scrambled, but Yuri ran up to the stage and lifted Malcom's head, placing it on her lap. Her friend was bleeding and having trouble breathing. He had been assassinated.

In the widely circulated *Life* magazine photo that captured that moment—Malcolm lying flat on the floor, his head on Yuri's lap—Yuri's name is missing.

"What did you say to him?" an interviewee asked Yuri, in 2006.

"I said, please, Malcolm, please, Malcolm—stay alive."[15]

Yuri's activism did not start and end with Malcolm, but friendships like his powered it. She worked and advocated for ethnic studies, political prisoners, Japanese American reparations, and against the Vietnam War. In 1977, she took over the Statue of Liberty with other Puerto Rican activists to raise awareness about the fight for Puerto Rican independence.

"What I will remember about Yuri Kochiyama," Professor Robyn Spencer said, "is her careful attention to mentoring and cultivating relationships."[16]

If you do not directly experience a particular injustice,

mustering enough care about it can feel dubious. Too abstract. It is why political action today often looks like "allyship," which has become superficial. The idea of allyship is like charity: doing something *for* others and not *with* others. Someone's suffering is made to feel separate from yours. Taking action is portrayed as self-sacrificial. Through friendship, however, what is otherwise distant turns urgent. Care becomes plentiful. Without friends, you might never take political action so long as your own interests are never endangered. With friends, whatever injustice arrives at their doorstep now implicates you too. Friendship carried June to causes around the world.

Even thousands of years ago, this is why friendship was considered dangerous. Between 384 and 379 BCE, Plato wrote, "The Persian empire is absolute; that is why it condemns love as well as philosophy and sport. It is no good for rulers if the people they rule cherish ambitions for themselves or form strong bonds of friendship with one another."[17]

When inequity thrives, friendship dies. When friendship thrives, inequity dies. The inequity in the Persian empire imperiled friendship. Today's inequities imperil friendship too, because inequity relies on the exploitation of many for the well-being of a few. If the many, however, started feeling responsible to pursue justice for their friends, for one another, then it would require deconstructing these institutions, and the inequities that they produce in their friends' lives. In other words, friendship would require justice.

Hence, the sparseness of political action, and the short-lived nature of it today, is traceable to the quality of friendship in our lives. With the loss of friendship today, we have also lost a critical pathway to justice.

Consider the recent #BlackLivesMatter movement. It had no headquarters but was shared and legitimized through social media. While the Internet allowed people to recruit strangers transnationally, self-organize cost-efficiently, break from traditional politics, and bring the leadership of three Black women to the forefront, it was also episodic and reactive. It was conducive to weaker online friendships and ties—relationships built on utility. We forgot that generations before us, the Civil Rights Movement, was highly organized and required a presence in the physical world, extensive underground training, strategy, and the commitment of thousands to one another. It required community. Friends. Not people as props in photos to be posted on Facebook, Instagram, Twitter, Snapchat, or Tik-Tok. Friends.

Alicia Garza, one of #BlackLivesMatter's founders, said, "Our aspiration should not be to have a million followers on Twitter. We shouldn't be focused on building a brand but building a base, and building the kind of movement that can succeed."[18]

Our world looks different when you recognize friendship's role in sculpting it. You notice friends' handprints everywhere. We are taught that social change looks like the latest iPhone, but the most significant social change is actually the ability to sit anywhere on a public bus, drink from any water fountain, or exist as you do today. It was not quantum leaps in space travel, but quantum leaps in human rights that have changed our lives most acutely today. It is not in a capitalist nation's interest to make people strive to participate in *this* type of social change—what is called social justice—because it is a direct challenge to itself, and the inequities that it yields.

If we recalibrate what we recognize as social change though, we notice something. The most remarkable social change you and I enjoy does not belong to Steve Jobs, but to friends who labored to create more equitable realities for us. Like June Jordan and her friends. Like Rosa Parks and her friend Johnnie Carr. Like Dr. Martin Luther King Jr. and his friend Ralph Abernathy. When Martin thundered out a fiery speech, Ralph would shuffle up to the podium afterward, saying, "Now, let me tell you what that means for tomorrow morning."[19] Martin's grandiose, inspiring remarks had to be supplemented by his friend's useful, albeit less glamorous, translations. We all need counterbalancing friendships like this.

Activism is not a nine to five job. Activism, just like friendship, consists of everyday acts that have bigger repercussions. This recognition yanks friendship into a realm of importance that we struggle imagining today. Most popular friendships of significance we know are fictional, like *Scooby-Doo*, *Harry Potter*, and *Percy Jackson*. In real life, friendships who defeat injustices are barely whispers. Not because they do not exist—political friendships have a strikingly bright history. They have just been erased, extracted from collective memory. Preventing us from remembering, as June Jordan writes, that "we are the ones we have been waiting for."[20]

5.

Laughing with Friends

TONI MORRISON SHARED a forty-plus-year friendship with public speaker, critic, and comedian Fran Lebowitz. Their friendship was instantaneous.

Fran said, "I don't know how to describe it, but it was like falling in love, except it lasted."[1]

Toni and Fran loved going to the movies. Standing outside a theater, someone in line behind them said, "I see you two together all the time. Are you related?"

Fran turned her head slowly. Toni was Black, Fran white, twenty years younger, and with signature cropped brown hair and circular glasses.

"Yes," Fran said. "She's my son."[2]

After Toni died, Fran said, "Here's a thing that most

people don't know about Toni: Toni was one of the most fun people I've ever known. And I am an expert on fun."[3]

The sole argument Toni and Fran had was whether Toni's apple pie was better than Fran's mother's apricot strudel, resolved only after they tasted and compared them both.[4] When Toni won the Nobel Prize, she invited Fran and others with her to Sweden, nicknaming them "Nobel-ettes," insisting that Fran stopped by her hotel room immediately after landing, because Toni needed help with her speech and with deciding what gloves to wear. Toni adored clothes, Fran explained. Gowns, gloves, all of it. When Toni was hospitalized after her hip replacement, most visitors brought her ruminative literature, like the early twentieth-century French author Marcel Proust—what else for a Nobel Prize winner? Fran, however—to the horror of one visitor from Princeton University, where Toni taught—brought Toni trashy tabloids.[5]

Like Toni, while you might seem serious at work, to your children, or to passersby, with friends, your icy exterior becomes powdered snow that you can play in. You roast friends lovingly, dote on, tease, and celebrate their quirks. You share playlists, new artists, and invite one another on adventures. While romantic and familial relationships are often exclusive, there are fewer limits with friendship. You can connect with more people from different backgrounds, opposite personalities, and curious tastes. Friends become portals to new, unexpected experiences, splattering fresh colors onto life's walls. You are a stranger to most in this world, but to your friends, you are you, and that itself is a joy.

Joy attracts us to friendship. It is its pull. Reading about the political friendships mentioned in this book, you might think, my friendships cannot become like them. My friendships are too goofy, and friendships conducive to more demanding dialogue, thinking, and action must require absolute seriousness. You might not feel like a serious, highbrow person. You might not envision yourself like Toni Morrison in some photos, sleeves rolled up, eyebrows scrunched, brainstorming how to disrupt the literary field. But maybe you can envision yourself like Toni dancing in a nightclub or waiting in line with her friend at the movies. Your conversations' severity is not an indication of whether your friendships can become more substantial or not. Joy is. The more your friendships are saturated with joy—the more laughter, inside jokes, silliness, giddy memories and spontaneity—the more qualified you are to wade through life's more serious sorrows together, too. And the more you will feel compelled to protect joy. Everything you love about friendship, all of its joyousness, is exactly what enables people to not only endure everyday struggles, but larger political ones too.

Good friendship is fun *and* deep, playful *and* accountable. We typically do not think of joy and sorrow as interrelated like this. Aristotle's "friendships of pleasure" frames joy entirely differently. Joy in "friendships of pleasure" have no relation to sorrow, so they remain superficial. Pleasure is unsustainable, unable to withstand the *un*pleasurable stuff of life. Friends leave as soon as things get hard.

Good friendship reframes pleasure as not only compatible with suffering, the *un*pleasant stuff in life, but inextricable from it, intimately a part of it.

This does not mean encouraging more sorrow in people's lives, or adopting a mindset that every good thing has a price, or what goes up must come down. It is instead a reminder that sorrow, inescapable as it is in human life, does not have conflicting interests with joy. Because good friendships are not only joyous. Maintaining friendship is hard work. Friends suffer from losing loved ones, heartbreak, layoffs, and illness. Caring for friends in a society that values some over others is particularly hard work that forces an awareness of inequities. None of this, however, negates the joy that you can feel.

Geologist Dr. Rainer Newberry coined two types of fun. "Type 1 fun" feels like fun in the moment. "Type 2 fun," however, might feel grueling in the moment, but it is fun in retrospect.[6] Like a group hike that scabs everyone's knees, but which you all finished nevertheless, the pride afterward proliferating. Similarly, friendship's sorrows do not always disqualify you from its joys. Sorrow does not pronounce you ineligible for joy. Sorrow brings people together, and the more chances to be together like that, raw, hurting, and vulnerable, the more chances for an unbridled, electrifying joy we have too.

When you have friends, you lose friends. When you fight with friends, you appreciate laughing with them more. Joy holds the hand of sorrow to stand upright, and vice versa.

In *The Prophet*, written in 1923, Lebanese American poet Khalil Gibran describes joy and sorrow as complementary: a cup of wine is made in a scolding hot oven; an enchanting musical instrument is carved by a knife's sharp edge. Sorrow is caused by what once, due to its presence, made you joyful, Gibran says. Joy is caused by what once, due to its absence, made you sorrowful.[7]

You should not feel guilty as you transform your friendships into more serious bonds. Joy is not the opposite of sorrow. Joy rushes in like ocean waves, traveling as deeply as our sorrow's cavities. You might think, like an overcrowded bus, if sorrow gets on, joy must get off. But joy and sorrow together push out the walls, making room for all of life's emotions.

In 44 BCE, the Roman statesman Cicero wrote, "For friendship adds a brighter radiance to prosperity and lessens the burden of adversity by dividing and sharing it."[8]

The more adversity is shared, the lighter it feels. And the more *joy* is shared, the heavier it feels, in a good way. Friendship buffers our sorrows, and it thickens our joys. A friend's listening ear lightens the load off you. Texting a friend your vacation photos, she too experiences the joy, amplifying it. We do not have to choose between only fun friendships and serious ones. Friendship reconciles both.

We forget joy and sorrow's relationship when thinking about activism. Activism is framed as rote, serious work. We use phrases like *"fighting* for justice," or *"struggling* for change." We see famous activists by a bus window, looking out in silence. Or leading a march, face stern. When we see these figures as individuals, we forget the joy. When we broaden the frame and see them as friends, the joy is indisputable. Because activists are just people and people, especially during tough times, must laugh a lot with friends.

In a 1989 essay called "The Dance of Revolution," June Jordan confesses to feeling burnout.

"Every once in a while, it happens. You can't even predict or block this ugly, overwhelming kind of thing," she writes. "Suddenly, you're writhing flat at the absolute bottom of your morale. Nothing important or good seems possible."

Reading about incessant global tragedies, tired from her own political activism, June felt defeated. She writes that when inundated with sorrow, "'What is to be done?' slurs into 'What difference does it make?'"

You must wait for a surprise, June says, to pick yourself back up. A surprise finally arrived when June's friends, filmmaker Pratibha Parmar and her partner Shaheen Haq, visited from England.

Pratibha and Shaheen stayed with June in her Brooklyn apartment. As a birthday present to Shaheen, June somehow secured tickets to a sold-out benefit concert, cohosted by Madonna. All three attended, waiting impatiently. Eventually Madonna and her cohost walked onstage in matching outfits. After sharing facts about murdered rainforests, "to the complete amazement of everyone present," June writes, "Madonna and Sandra Bernhard then clasped hands, and in each other's arms, sang..."

June had never seen anything like it in her life. She could not breathe. The London *Daily Sun* wrote about the event, "The Love Birds...stunned an audience with their lesbian romp."

June leaped to her feet, clapping with the audience, with

her friends, exhilarated. It "astounded and aroused [June's] sleeping heart."[9]

Pratibha told me, "June knew both of us were big Madonna fans at the time. We were all so high and couldn't stop beaming and laughing."

Every single one of June's friends I spoke to would look afar, unprompted, and describe June's laughter: a full-body giggle that peppered most of her words. One friend, writer E. Ethelbert Miller, said he and June would attend serious political meetings, but would get caught laughing in a corner, passersby shaking their heads, saying, you two are like kids! Another friend, poet, cultural worker, and educator Kathy Engel, described participating in an intense political event with June, hosted by a congressman. On a walk afterward, June stopped, looked at the hills, and asked, is this a hike? Would this be considered a hike?

"And we all cracked up, it was just so perfect," Kathy said. "It was like, I don't know, is it a hike? Having been in this serious, serious place, we'd done this groundbreaking work with the congressman, and then we're debating whether this is considered a hill, or a mountain, or a hike. We had a lot of moments like that as friends."

Author and illustrator Alexis De Veaux told me that June would call her, fuming, enraged by something—"I'm gonna kill so-and-so!"—so Alexis would run over to June's apartment, gradually getting her to laugh about it, calming her down. Embodied joy is so important to our resistances, Alexis said, because it "releases the steam of multiple oppressive pressures." It alleviates all the heaviness. It lets us breathe. It makes the fight feel good, not only good, but makes resistance work "the most pleasurable experiences we can have on this planet," as author adrienne maree brown says, too.[10]

We never learn about this side of famous friendships, the fun, joyous side, but we must. The more we do, the more we can recognize ourselves in them. You might think your silly friendships cannot possibly be as sophisticated as those rigorous political ones, but they are more than you know.

Friendship remedies even the worst, most sorrowful day. You can spin almost any sadness into an entertaining tale for your friends—that time you lost your passport while traveling, that time you got your heart broken, that time you were robbed. It is perhaps why, in our capitalist economy, happy hours are systematically encouraged after workdays: drinking and socializing with friends helps even the most overworked and underpaid worker return to work the next morning.

Black feminist and theorist bell hooks—who uncapitalized her pen name to minimize individual identity—was good friends with Iranian American scholar and activist

M. Shadee Malaklou. Often, bell would call Dr. Malaklou a "'prophet of doom,' someone who thought too critically at the expense of [her] joy."

Together though, the two friends "laughed, and laughed, and laughed," Dr. Malaklou writes. "We sifted through boxes of magazines, scouring them for positive images of black, brown, and queer women, and window shopped on Etsy for Turkish rugs. Giggling with bell in the living room, kitchen, and hallways of her home, as she spilled the tea, disabused me of my pessimism."[11]

Friendship's joyousness is a rocket flare illuminating the faces around us during those endless nights. Recall a great concert you heard with a friend, or a good meal you shared. Friendship's joyousness inspires you, reignites you, dissipating your dreariness. Our ability to laugh with friends, even during the toughest of times, soothes our weariness and simplifies what matters: right now, this, you. Joy is a human spiritual indispensability. Laughter's radiance recharges us, reenlisting us into the struggle of everyday life. This is why friendship is so feared. This is why capitalism depends on control and disconnection.

Joy gives us something to fight for, not just against. Joy guides us, even if experienced for only a minute, on a hike, talking on the phone with a friend, or passing them on your way to a meeting. When we feel joy through our friendships, we can feel where we lack it, and then we can try changing those areas of lack.

Words like "allyship" and images of social movements often have no lusciousness; in Kathy Engel's words, "no jazz, delight, or warmth to them." They are uninviting. Friendship makes resistance tolerable, if not irresistible, through the joy that it spreads. Admitting that joy is the heartbeat of social movements is what invites us back into them.

Civil Rights activist Jo Ann Robinson saw Dr. Martin Luther King Jr. happiest after he delivered a keynote in Alabama. Unable to attend the dinner-dance afterward, he called the venue. Someone interrupted Jo Ann, mid-dancing. She walked over to the phone, attached to the dance floor's wall. Hello? Martin asked if his church members were in attendance. Jo Ann looked around and said yes. He asked if she would hand the phone to them "as they danced by."

"He was completely happy during that time. I could hear him laughing as he talked, though I did not hold the receiver," Jo Ann recalls. "It took only little things such as this to make him happy. I attributed his happiness that night to camaraderie: good will and friendship."[12]

Relationships, whether you call yourself a good friend, activist, organizer, or curator, are the core of movements that effect change. If not for each other, the joyous moments we share, the laughter that makes our bellies ache, then what are we fighting for? If not love, then what else?

What is more, structures of inequity make it so that wealthy white men have the greatest access to joy. Since the world is structured around mass joylessness, if more people felt entitled to experience joy, it would mean restructuring the world—more joy would mean more liberation. Meaning, your joy is not selfish, but actually improves the world.[13] And the surest way for you to feel joy, is through friendship.

6.

Making Friends

A POPULAR AND comical measure of a friendship is the question, will you help me bury a body? Good friends, so it goes, are unquestioning. They show up with a shovel.

After college, I moved to San Francisco and made new friends. I met people through word of mouth, through friends of friends of friends. I went on friend dates in coffee shops, restaurants, museums, and parks overlooking the hilly city.

A familiar claustrophobia closed in.

My friendships were forming around college degrees.

I went out to eat with these new friends one rainy night. Wringing out her wet hair, Sylvia admitted being financially tight after a recent big purchase she made. Concern leaped into my chest. Another friend slapped her card down on the bill, saying she would cover Sylvia's portion. If friendship was not a core value in this group, we might not have helped beyond words of encouragement and a listening ear (or, without a Venmo request).

Many of our friendships are based on likeness, people perceived to be the same as us, because of their class, race, gender, sexuality, or another social marker like college pedigree, as my new friends were. For people facing the brunt of injustice, likeness is refreshing. Explaining yourself is unnecessary in a world where you constantly need to. It is an act of self-preservation, too. As a woman of color, befriending other women of color at work can mean ensuring no one falls behind in a system designed against her progress.

But when people with more social power and capital create friendships based on likeness, friendship can become exclusive. The promise of showing up with a shovel becomes dangerous.

At Ivy League universities, one in every six students has a parent in the top 1 percent.[1] The other five sixths benefit from advantageous prospects: Ivy League alumni, on average, "earn substantially more than graduates from other four-year universities."[2] In this setting, while friendship ideally disrupts individualism, pulling you further toward community, friendships in privileged circles do not pull you that far. Being a good friend to *only* your friends is what ensures the wealthy stay wealthy. Rather than disrupting social divides, friendship fortifies them, fluffing the cushions underneath the already cushioned.

Friends that are likely to understand you are also unlikely to challenge you. We need good friendships that are cross-class, interracial, gender diverse, and so on, but friendships among the more privileged often involve friends of equal "caliber." Care does expand beyond your own self-interest, but it circulates within cliques without the direst need of that care. My friend Sylvia was tight on cash, after all, because her big purchase was a luxury cruise to Thailand. As I watched the card go down, looking at the faces around that restaurant table, then outside, into the rainy city, at the dozens of nameless faces, I remember wondering, does being a good friend matter if this is as big as my friendships' impact gets?

In two recent studies led by Harvard economist Professor Raj Chetty, researchers concluded that wealthy children in the US live in neighborhoods where 70 percent of their friends are also wealthy. If poor children grew up with the same number of wealthy friends, it would raise their future incomes by 20 percent on average.[3]

"These cross-class friendships—what the researchers called economic connectedness—had a stronger impact than school quality, family structure, job availability or a community's racial composition," writes the *New York Times.* "The people you know, the study suggests, open up opportunities, and the growing class divide in the United States closes them off."[4]

Making friendships across class lines is not just a matter of personal preference, or simply deciding to befriend people across economic brackets. It is not singularly up to you, a matter of shifting your mindset—it also requires structural changes, including improving limited access to universities, lack of affordable housing, and inequitable school district designations, as Chetty says.[5]

Yet, where we *can* individually make decisions that diversify our friend groups, we should. We should unlearn biases zapping us to familiar privileges, and we should avoid passively riding friendship currents that lock us inside identical circles. Instead, we can be active about making friendships, deepening and intensifying them with intention. At the very least, this can look like explicitly discussing finances with good friends, ensuring activities in your shared calendars can be afforded by everybody, and so on. These good friendships are harder, but they are politically vital. Actively rattling likeness is how friendships avoid becoming insular, whether because of your class or other privileges, like race (three out of four white people have no nonwhite friends).[6] And token diverse friends will not help you. Good friendship repels tokenization, because it is steadfast and deep, the opposite of tokenization, which is extractive and reductive.

Friendship's goodness is supposed to lie in how it grows care beyond limited self-interest, helping us become better, more community-oriented people. But if you are good to only *your* friends, bad to everyone else, friendship is not necessarily a good thing. The ripple-effects of good friendship are meek. Friendship does not challenge your self-interest. It only functions like a boomerang, returning to you, ultimately securing your self-interest.

Friendship *is* powerful. It *can* grow your care, but how much is up to you. It *can* become the basis of a movement, but what kind of movement is undetermined. Friendships drove the abolitionist movement, Civil Rights Movement, feminist movements, and others, but friendship crescendos in histories of injustice, too. Friendship is not faultless. Just because you do something in friendship's name, does not make it inherently good.

Cronyism, similar to nepotism, is a kind of friendship. A wink to a buddy, the opening of a door to an undeserving friend. Cronyism's etymology goes back to the seventeenth century: "crony" was used by the University of Cambridge's students as slang for "friend." Crony*ism* now conveys when friends are given preferential treatment based on their familiarity, or likeness, not their merit.[7]

Friendship thrived in the Ku Klux Klan, too. Members of the Women's Ku Klux Klan were motivated by white supremacy, yes, but also by friendship and protecting a shared way of life. One Klan member even pretended ignorance about the Klan's broader actions; for her, growing up in rural Indiana, the Klan was just "a way to get together and enjoy" with other white Protestant women.[8]

Friendship is not inherently a good thing. Friendships, if we are not careful, can perpetuate harm. Looking around our dinner tables, we should ask, Who are my friends? And why? Sometimes relationships, in the name of friendship, can actually trap us into exclusive bonds limited by likeness.

No two people are exactly alike. As two Asian Americans who lived in a predominantly white neighborhood, my friend Ryan and I felt alike. Then, at a concert, I felt *un*like Ryan as he pushed through crowds with an air of invincibility, because of his privileges as a cisgender man. We again felt alike visiting our parents' home countries, because of our American accents and passports; however, back in the US, Ryan felt unlike me because he is a child of refugees, while I am a child of immigrants.

Good friendship inevitably reveals the penetrability of

likeness, how social categories are relative but not factual. No two people are the same, and presuming so risks concealing friends or burying vital differences between them, keeping friendships surface level. If Ryan and I were friends in one context, like a science experiment with all variables controlled, we might suppose we are alike. But as we spend more time together, and variables change, we change too. Likeness is an unsustainable connector. Good friendship unmasks people's dimensionality and pushes us toward communing for reasons deeper than likeness.

June Jordan writes, "I am wondering if those of us who began our lives in difficult conditions defined by our race or our class or our gender identities, I am wondering if we can become more carefully aware of the limitations of race and gender analyses, for these yield only distorted and deeply inadequate images of ourselves.

"There is another realm of possibility: political unity and human community based on concepts that underlie or supersede relatively immutable factors of race, class, and gender: the concept of justice, the concept of equality, the concept of tenderness."[9]

Nobody can only fight for their friends to win. White feminists cannot aspire to replacing the patriarchy with only cisgender white women. Asian Americans cannot replace white supremacy with Asian Americans over everyone else. This only changes inequity's flavor, not its roots.

We need people unlike us as friends. When resisting anti-Black racism, other people of color and white people must resist too. Movements need numbers for effectiveness, and multiracial groups can leverage their power to keep Black protestors safe. Just as, when resisting transphobic violence, cisgender people must resist. We find refuge in friendships with people like us, but for our own sakes, we should venture to build friendships beyond likeness. We should seek friends who, no matter how unalike, are alike in their determination to be good friends. We should exchange friendships based on likeness for friendships based on a like-mindedness: that in every stranger rests the possibility of friendship.

Still, even if you do challenge likeness in your friendships, is friendship *inherently* an exclusive act? You cannot befriend everybody, so, in order to face a friend, must you turn your back on others? After all, snapping a photo of friends, you exclude everyone outside the frame.

Aristotle believed friendship "decreased in quality as it increased in quantity," as author Mary Hunt writes. He thought "the more intense the friendship, the fewer people with whom it was possible to enjoy it."[10]

Yet, while good friendship *is* rare, the ethics of good friendship are not. Friendship, depending on how you practice it, can help you love *one person in particular,* or it can help you love *people.* You do not need Olympian levels of extroverted-ness to accomplish the latter, either.

June was walking her dog in North Berkeley, California, when suddenly a young white man ran toward her. An antisemitic book had been dropped onto his front lawn twice that day. He lived with his wife, who was Jewish, and their newborn baby. He asked if June had seen anything or anyone suspicious.

June said no, and she asked the man, Eric, how he was doing. She listened, gave Eric her name, phone number, and the numbers of "some active people who might rally, fast, against this hatefulness."

Being a good friend is not an inherently exclusive act. You can be a good friend to your friends, and to complete strangers too, like June was to Eric when in need. Friendship can shrivel your care or expand it, if you allow the growth. Friendships can escalate into dangerous cliques, *or* good friendships—ones that responsibly engage and disengage with likeness—can ease us into unlatching from mandated loyalties to our supposedly inherent affiliations.

After June helped Eric, he invited her to meet his wife and child.

"But I never had the time," June writes. "Or, I never made the time to visit them."[11]

June was not friends with everyone, because she did not have to be. They say you are the average of the five people you spend the most time with. What you water, grows. Everyone will not be your friend, but everyone will benefit from the person you become through your good friendships.

In our highly individualistic society, how else could we develop the muscles required to connect with strangers, if we do not practice loving friends first, people who were once strangers? We cannot stop at friendship, but we must begin there. It was likely that through good friendship June managed to be not only a good friend to *her* friends, but even to the loneliest stranger on the other side of the planet, whether in North Berkeley, Brooklyn, Mississippi, South Africa, Nicaragua, Israel, Lebanon, Northern Ireland, or Palestine.[12] In this way, while friendship has been used for centuries to keep doors closed, to keep wealth inside certain people's safes, it can be used by us, too. Not friendship weaponized by people in power, but rather exercised by us, for our own liberation.

Friendship catapults us toward collectivity in a society where even the association of *one new person* is tricky, unpracticed. When reaching broader solidarities, however, we find our footing with friendship. Good friendship is about extending your love to another, and then another, and then another. It is not accumulation. It is about developing an ethic of care—care to the extent of risking your own privilege for someone—that ultimately has consequences beyond the well-being of that someone.

Dr. Cornel West has said that justice is what love looks like in public, and to reach that level, we start with friendship. Friendship is not inherently exclusive. To be the friend of one, does not necessarily make you the enemy of another. Friendship can be an end in and of itself but also a means to a larger end, one where your care for people apart from yourself swells, like ink bleeding into water.

7.

Bad Friendship

FRIENDSHIP IS OFTEN riddled with disappointment. Mid-nineteenth century American writer Ralph Waldo Emerson believed that most people "descend to meet," tumbling downward into mundane, disappointing relationships.

"The very flower and aroma of the flower of each of the beautiful natures disappears as they approach each other," Emerson writes.

Every interaction with a friend becomes a "compromise."

"Solitude" alone relieves you.[1]

If you expect friendship to lack conflict, you will become disappointed. If you see conflict as inevitable, your disappointment recedes. Because friendships are only perfect if kept aloof, like romantic crushes—perfect through distance's illusion. If you welcome uneasiness, you welcome friends to come sit close. You understand that, when two people come together, it is natural that small, fiery particles are thrown off from their collision.

It is October 13, 1989, in a photograph I am looking at and, momentarily, June Jordan and Adrienne Rich will speak at the National Poetry Festival together. They are preparing, seated side by side in a shadowed corner. Behind them, the room steadily radiates sunlight. Their table has a flair of artistic disarray: cups of water, plates, napkins, and books sprinkled about. June reads a thick black text, her head down, chin slanted upward, eyebrow slightly arched. Adrienne, one of the most public and widely read poets of the second half of the twentieth century, has her elbows tucked in, her right wrist in motion, jotting notes in a journal stacked atop more books. They appear content, relaxed, snug in the comfortable silence that old friends rhythmically melt into.[2]

June first met Adrienne when she was colleagues with Adrienne's husband, Alfred H. Conrad, at the City College of New York. After Alfred died, Adrienne knocked on June's door in Brooklyn. June did not recognize her. Adrienne had become a lesbian separatist. There was a newfound engagement with Adrienne's racialized and gendered identity that June admired, a particular relentlessness to examine "pivotal questions that torment contemporary life."[3] They started meeting weekly, eating regularly at an Indian restaurant on Ninety-Third Street, exchanging poems. They became friends.

In 1982, Israel invaded Lebanon. Around this time, Adrienne publicly asserted that she was a Jewish lesbian and a Zionist. A letter "Anti-Zionism is Anti-Semitism" circulated nationally in feminist press, and June saw Adrienne's name among the seven signees. Neither in her prose, poetry, or personally to June did June notice Adrienne verbalize her Jewishness before.

June said, "It would be like if Idi Amin," the military dictator of Uganda who killed an estimated three hundred thousand civilians during his presidency, "was rampaging, as he did, and until then I had never identified myself as Black."[4]

June challenged Adrienne on moral grounds and submitted her thoughts to the same publication that had published Adrienne's "Anti-Zionism is Anti-Semitism." They refused her. Adrienne is the mother of our movement, they said. We cannot go against her. So June mailed it directly to Adrienne.

June's friend Alexis De Veaux told me, "I would not want to present June in a way that doesn't allow for her deep humanity, especially as her friend. She could be messy.

She was as wounded as any of us, and those wounds may have seeped into moments when she got angry at you. You could be her friend on Tuesday, then not her friend on Thursday. It could be lethal."

Adrienne did not respond.[5]

Conflict in friendship does not always look dramatic. Often, it is subtler. You forget friends' birthdays; you forget to text back. You are caught saying yes to a romantic partner, but no to friends. You shout at each other; you are passive-aggressive. You ignore each other, before finding your way back. Intimacy is predicated on the realization that I can hurt you. That you can hurt me. Even for the most remarkable friendships in history, friendship was messy, unpleasant, and often tense.

Friendship is a neglected bond. Nobody prepares us to be friends. There are no templates, no guidebooks. Messing up is guaranteed because friendship is improvisational. It takes a lot of bad friendship to become a good friend.

In 1982, June visited Palestinian refugee camps after the massacre of Sabra and Shatila.[6] The architecture of the entrapment relied heavily on cement. Cables danced above, swinging from balcony to balcony. Bodies filled the streets. Children walked aghast among them, shielding their nostrils with their T-shirts.

In a poem "Moving towards Home," June writes, "I do

not wish to speak about the bulldozer and the / red dirt / not quite covering all of the arms and legs..." She finishes writing, "I was born a Black woman / and now / I am become a Palestinian..."[7]

An attack on anyone felt personal to June. Nobody's well-being was a competing interest. If the world was silent about anyone's oppression, the world was capable of being silent about the oppression of Black people—of any people—down the line. This is why, traveling the world, June observed "pivotal connections" between otherwise "disparate victories, or among apparently disparate events of suffering, and loss."[8] And why June felt she had become a Palestinian. Why, after a member of the Aryan Nation attacked a Los Angeles Jewish community center, searching for Jewish people with his semiautomatic gun, June visited and published a piece on the horror, ending it defiantly with, "Are you hunting for Jews? You're looking for me!"[9]

But this was not Adrienne's world. Adrienne instead believed Virginia Woolf's sentiment that "as a woman I have no country. As a woman I want no country. As a woman, my country is the whole world." Woolf published those words in 1938, during the height of the British Empire. Her country *was* the whole world.

Adrienne used Woolf's ethic to warrant a similar kind of evasiveness years later as an American, one that June detected, but did not comprehend the extent of, until Adrienne's public support of Israel in 1982.[10]

Years of silence elapsed between June and Adrienne.

"During the interim I understand that, among other things, she went to Nicaragua," June said.[11]

In Nicaragua, Adrienne's worldview expanded, becoming more internationalist. In a University of Massachusetts, Amherst talk around this time, Adrienne admits that she once would have recited Woolf's lines "without second thought," but now she realized that they should not be used to "justify a false transcendence, an irresponsibility toward the cultures and geo-political regions in which we are rooted."[12]

After around three years, June ran into Adrienne at an anti-apartheid poetry reading.

When separated from friends, they can turn into unbending, two-dimensional, villainous shadows. Seeing them in-person, the clouds part.

Experiencing and surviving disagreements over time, accepting friendship as a relation that ebbs and flows, helps us not over-dramatize conflict, not see it as catastrophic or necessarily polarizing. As the artist group Raqs Media Collective writes, "agreements and disagreements" do not have to "cancel each other out in a zero-sum game," but can instead blend into "new levels of connectedness."[13]

June walked toward Adrienne. She said in one breath, "I completely and absolutely detest your views on Israel and I love you."

Adrienne stood.

They embraced.

Later, Adrienne asked June to forgive her.[14]

When conflict erupts, our friendships often sink into a reality muted in color. The bond is dropped, shattering, and we withdraw from the friendship. But conflict can strengthen a relationship. Conflict does not make your friendship lackluster, but more vibrant every time—if it improves from it.

"By 1956, I had begun dating each of my poems by year," Adrienne said. "I knew my life was changing, my work was changing, and I needed to indicate to readers my sense of being engaged in a long, continuing process."[15]

Her friendships were vital in her growth. Friends and peers like Toni Cade Bambara, Ama Ata Aidoo, Dionne Brand, Judy Grahn, Audre Lorde, Nancy Morejón, and June Jordan. Even in her absence, I believe Adrienne felt June's presence, her challenge.

Adrienne became involved with organizations advocating for Palestinians, like the New Jewish Agenda, and continued taking political action for Palestinians until the end of her life.[16] It was not one-sided, with her more marginalized friends educating her, only for her benefit. Resolving conflict is not about apologizing and skating over issues. It is about transformation. Friendship makes challenge intimate and painfully direct. How you change is what you give back, and for your friend, that future you is worth struggling for.

Friendships that are well-oiled machines, mechanically good and happy, operate at a distance. The farther away you stand, the less details and imperfections our eyes catch. As you become closer, you experience not a descension into reality, as Emerson would say, but an honest complication of reality. It is only natural. We are lenient toward romantic partners and family, normalizing that "love takes work" with them, but not with friends. We gift our family hundreds of second chances, but we drop friends at the first sign of trouble. In doing so, we keep our friends at arm's length. We scratch friendship's surface, retreating whenever tension bubbles.

Choosing to *stay* in the friendship reveals your respect for the bond. If we pull friendship into a central status, not a peripheral one, then we give friends the same grace. The same patience. Insisting that they are not replaceable, that they are worth the trouble, because our friends are just as important.

Most translations of Aristotle's superior category of

friendship, "friendships of virtue," translate the phrase as "perfect friendship." Perfectly virtuous friends, Aristotle says, arrive at their friendships without a speck of dust, unquestionably good.[17] He believed friendships should be pristine bonds. But friendship is not utopic. Sometimes, it is *through* friendship that we discover our goodness. Sometimes, two imperfect people workshop their values, character, and dispositions, aspiring for perfection together.

Am I too adoring of friendship? Am I writing through the haze of romanticization? Should friendship's painfulness sober my views? I think about this often. When I raised these concerns to the professor advising my undergraduate research on friendship, Dr. Eddie Glaude, he reminded me that there is no pristine place from which to practice friendship, nor from which to love. Friendship's painfulness might curb our hopes for it. But I sense that friendship's complexity, the pain *and* refuge within it, still supports a revolutionary proposition: friendship as center stage—not a bland relation merely accessorizing romantic or familial ones. Friendship as good, bad, and everything in between. Friendship as not black-and-white, but as intricately complex as any relation.

Conflict can be toxic, and sometimes we *should* step away from friendships, but we should not make that decision callously. Too often, we prioritize easy friendships, and if it becomes hard, we evaluate the bond's necessity. We prefer friends to distract us from the hard stuff, not to *be* the hard stuff. But conflict is not a failure, deep relationship-ing makes it inevitable. Since we never learn how to be friends, we try, experiment, fail, and try again within our friendships, often in real-time. I try to make my peace with that learning and unlearning. We should normalize that friendship is an oscillating, ever-changing, fluid process filled with hit or missed experiences. Friendships are good, and sometimes they are not. Good friendship is a practice, not a destination.

8.

Friendship with Men

A MAN NAMED E. Ethelbert Miller proposed to June Jordan.

They did not get married, however, because June "really felt that I would need to have children," Ethelbert told me. He had kind eyes, a racing mind, and laughed easily. "June was not having children anymore. And she felt that it was something that I needed to experience. She was a friend that helped me make that decision, someone who cared about me so much that she realized, okay, for you to reach your full potential as a person, you need to be a father."

I might once have dismissed their relationship as a failed romantic relationship since it did not culminate in marriage. But June said no not from a place of rejection, but from a place of redirection—not back toward friendship, as though friendship was a setback in a relationship's development, but forward toward it.

Can men and women be friends? Unless you are un-attracted or unavailable, we are generally taught, no. In movies like *When Harry Met Sally*, we see that men and women must be romantically and sexually involved for it to mean anything, constantly toeing a will-they-won't-they dynamic. But this is often just a "narrative problem," as author William Deresiewicz writes. Friendship does not obviously have "a beginning, a middle, and an end."[1] No big wedding, no first kiss. We do not yet know how to tell the story of friendship, how to identify its moments of suspense, connection, and commitment. So, all relationships are forced into a romance on the big screen.

We also lack popular narratives about friendships between men and women because of patriarchy, which delineates two genders, each with a narrow set of roles. Imposed definitions about what it means to be a "man" and "woman" in today's society muck up friendships, too.

A "subject" is a person or thing who *does* something. An "object" is a person or thing who has something being done *to* it. In the sentence "I took the car." "I" is the subject, the person doing something, and "car" is the object, the thing having something done to it. In our patriarchal world, women become object-like. It is why we feminize cars and other inanimate objects—saying, "Do you like my car? Isn't she gorgeous?" And why women are objects of men's desire: men are the ones who ask women out, propose, etcetera.

But women are not born objects. The reality of being a woman in a patriarchal world, how you are socialized, makes it so. From a young age, girls are objectified; at the mercy of this world's self-made subjects (men). It is why, as research shows, women tend to put others' needs first.[2] You become adept at assessing your likability and catering to others in order to stay safe and feel accepted. This is also why women say sorry and give compliments more than men; why women ask for what they want less than men;[3] why, to minimize assertiveness, women lift their speaking tones at the ends of sentences as if asking a question. You find yourself—even if not sexually or romantically attracted to men—seeking men's validation. Does he think I am pretty? Is he having a good time? Is he enjoying our conversation?

Friendship, however, must be between two subjects, not a subject and an object. In *Nicomachean Ethics*, Aristotle explains how you can love objects, but you cannot befriend objects. You can love wine, but you cannot befriend wine.[4] Friendship requires reciprocity, a mutuality. It is about verbs: the *act* of loving, and the *receiving* of another's love, not about what is "lovable." It is about relationship, not association.

For men and women to be friends, both people need subjecthood. Or at least, equitable efforts for both to *feel* the dignity of subjecthood within their friendship. Subjecthood means reciprocity, which is key to friendship. You can say you are in love with someone, or that you love something, even if the other party is unaware, even if it is nonreciprocal. You cannot, however, say that you are someone's friend without them knowing it, too.

As a woman, you might start friendships with men who you are romantically and sexually uninterested in, only to realize that, down the road, something romantic or sexual is expected. It feels dehumanizing, because it is. You are an object: not a person, but a body first. Unpracticed at seeing women as full people, cis straight men often misplace the intimacy they feel in their friendships with women. Friendship is unimaginable because women's subjecthood is too.

In one study, eighty-eight undergraduate friendship pairs consisting of one man and woman were separated and asked questions. Their answers remained confidential, particularly to each other. Men participants were more attracted to their women friends than vice versa. They were also more likely to think their women friends were attracted to them. Women were generally not attracted to friends who were men and "assumed that this lack of attraction was mutual." Men, on the other hand, desired friends who were women "regardless of their relationship status," while women were more "sensitive to their male friends' relationship status and uninterested in pursuing those who were already involved with someone else."[5]

I remember when my friend Andrea's guy friends disappeared.

"What happened?" I asked.

"I got a boyfriend."

Friendship was a charade. Her guy friends had presumed romance or sex was around the corner. When that illusion was disrupted, so, too, was the relationship.

A woman is not only meaningful if romantically or sexually possessed. If subjecthood is the goal of friendship, women are valued as friends, not only as romantic or sexual objects. We have pejorative terms like "friendzoned," but friendship is not a sidelined potential romance. People should not insist, "Why don't you just date each other?" Friendship is not a prelude to coupledom. It is not all or nothing. Friendship is meaningful in and of itself.

Good friends are emotionally intelligent enough to not confuse platonic intimacy as necessarily romantic. They understand platonic bonds, cherish them for what they are, and protect them, instead of mangling them into something they are not. My friend Anthony befriended a coworker who identifies as a woman. He respects their relationship as platonic—and not only because she has a boyfriend. Although others tease that "just because there is a goalie, does not mean you cannot score," he would never cross their mutually established boundaries. Working toward mutual subjecthood in friendships, he knows his desires should not supplant a woman's comfort.

An aspiration for mutual subjecthood will not only help friendships between men and women, but between men, too. The question "can men and women be friends" presupposes that friendships between men are easier. But in a patriarchal society, men also have trouble being friends with other men.

Men are in a "friendship recession"; one in five single men report having no close friends at all.[6] Their friendships run out of steam quickly. You might have tennis friends, poker friends, video game friends, but no friends you can be your full self with, no friends to emotionally unravel to without your masculinity unraveling, too. Instead, patriarchy and its gender roles stigmatize intimacy between men, keeping them from holding hands, draping arms around friends' shoulders, and from saying I love you. Instead, emotional labor is reserved for women. During times of need, women are many men's "first pick" to talk to, never guy friends. This again twists women into objects, expecting them to do the bulk of emotional work for you. It also skyrockets loneliness in men (your girlfriend cannot be your only confidant).

There are other ways to be. Queer people are unshy about probing at unspoken gender norms since our very existence does.

During the late 1970s, Alexis De Veaux and her then-girlfriend organized Sunday salons. They were inspired by the Harlem Renaissance of the early 1900s, a time when Black artists threw "rent parties" to socialize and sell food and drink to help pay the rent.

Alexis told me, "We believed that there were Black and brown queer women, women who identified as lesbian, who did not have the same kind of social outlets as white women, like bars or public spaces to go to."

During one salon in Harlem, June arrived with a lover. She was dressed "immaculately." Alexis did not know June, but knew of her, and she watched June have a good time. Eventually, Alexis moved to Brooklyn, where she found a larger apartment for her Sunday salons, and June moved from Manhattan to Brooklyn too, down the street from Alexis.

Alexis developed a "serious crush" on June.

"I did feel rejected and inadequate," Alexis told me,

when her crush was unreciprocated. "I would be lying if I said I didn't. But I also understood fairly quickly that June was offering me *so much more.*"

June stretched Alexis's imagination.

"Sex was not something that she needed from me, or that I particularly needed from her," Alexis said. "You know, there's a line in, I forget which Toni Morrison book it was, where the narrator says she was a friend *to my mind.* June was a friend *to my mind,* and I was a friend to hers. What you can actually offer a person is more than sex.

"June said, now, let's not do that [romantic and sexual stuff]. You can do that with somebody and I can do that with somebody, but we won't do that together. We got something else going on. And it's just as important."

In queer communities, terms like "queerplatonic partnership," meaning a committed nonromantic relationship, and "squish," meaning a platonic crush, seek to diversify our mental repertoire. Although such labels can become reductive too, they do succeed at stirring our imaginations. Anyone, whether you identify as queer or not, can take this initiative. You can queer—or trouble, diverge from the status quo, and shake up—*how* you do friendships, freeing your friendships from society's limiting roles.

Women today are socialized to practice friendships face-to-face, while men are socialized to practice friendships side by side.[7] Meaning, women commonly experience friendship by talking with one another, while men typically do activities together. Neither mode of friendship is inherently bad, but confining them based on your gender is. It is like the five love languages, created by Dr. Gary Chapman: words of affirmation, quality time, physical touch, receiving gifts, and acts of service. People like to focus on their top love language, when really, most need fulfillment across all realms. Similarly, we need both face-to-face *and* side by side friendship-ing to feel fulfilled in friendship.

Side by side friendships are activity-based, which, for men, causes confusing physical proximity for emotional proximity. Instead, men should place higher value on face-to-face friendships. Doing so undermines patriarchy, which prefers men quiet and divorced from their emotions—being out of touch with your emotions lays the groundwork for oppression; if you are emotionally stunted, you are less compassionate, and thus, more willing to hurt others and ignore harm when you see it in progress. Being emotionally transparent, on the other hand, means not only caring for yourself better, but also for other people. More intimacy leads to more emotional fluency, which leads to more compassion for people unlike you.

I spoke to Anthony because although he is cisgender and straight, his friendship with another cis straight man named Kevin aspires to be non-patriarchal. To shake up gender norms. Currently twenty-three and twenty-four, Anthony and Kevin have been friends since kindergarten. They say I love you. They kiss each other on the cheek. They talk about their feelings. With their other friends who are men, they attempt destigmatizing this emotional vulnerability, too. They do not over-celebrate it by giving it a special name—it is not a "bromance"—but try to normalize it as what normal healthy friendships look like.

At a recent get-together, Anthony said to his guy friends, "I just want to let you guys know, I'm interested in everything and anything you guys have to say. Let me know what is on your mind, how you are feeling. You can share anything with me."

On the other hand, for women, having only face-to-face friendships can be damaging too. I am learning to release my friends who are women from the emotional labor society demands we perform, even for other women. Although I often divulge to friends through talking, I am learning how sometimes actions speak louder than words. Sometimes, my friends can learn things about me that even *I* do not know about myself being by my side, doing activities like camping, dancing, or traveling. Activity-based friendships offer the chance to show, not tell. Face-to-face friendships can keep friendships tangential, always catching up, never becoming the main site of action themselves.

June's friendship nurtured Alexis intellectually and politically, through dialogue, but also literally. Through action. When Alexis had no money, she dialed June.

"Not only did June buy me food, but she came over with a bag of what she knew were my *favorite* foods. Tofu, scallions, avocado, good bread, pasta, all the things that she knew made me really happy."

Their friendship, although deep in conversation and face-to-face intimacy, gained dimension from its side by side intimacy. Alexis grew not just from June's conversations, but through her example. They did not stop at theory, they ventured into practice. *Doing* things together is what Alexis credits much of her activism today to.

Society wants us to believe that gender is factual. If we think it is strictly biological, without any social influence, we will not question it. If we do not question it, we allow gender constructs to block growth, as individuals and as a collective. We buy into the myth that there are only two gender identities, and that men are naturally like this, women are naturally like that—not because of how they are raised, but because of something immutable inside.

When we unlearn gender socialization, following in queer and trans communities' footsteps, we can resist rules and restrictions that pervert good friendship. That person you feel a connection with, consider, are your feelings actually romantic/sexual, *or* can you simply not yet imagine another meaningful way to be in relationship with them? If you dismiss them, because you cannot romantically or sexually claim them, you could be dismissing the best friendship of your life.

Moving beyond gender roles slashes arbitrary ceilings from our friendships. This is perhaps how June built good friendships with both Alexis and Ethelbert, friendships that escaped crushing gender norms. While all that open sky can feel scary, your friendships will soar higher. They will grow in favor of more clarity and communication about our bonds, rather than gender-based anxiety. They will grow more bravery too, to construct kinder, more honest and dignified doorways to one another.

9.

Love

AT THE ALTAR, brides and grooms confess to being best friends. Your other half is a balm to individualism and loneliness, a solution to all your unmet social desires. Marriage replaces many relationships, and the spouse becomes your friend, cohabitor, confidant, muse, and lover. But one person cannot fulfill what an entire community is meant to. One person cannot paradoxically be both your sense of security and also your sense of adventure, as psychotherapist Esther Perel says.[1] One person cannot be your everything friend.

We are compelled into rigid romantic structures nonetheless through taxation, healthcare, housing benefits, lack of social stigma, cultural security, and an overall ease moving through the world with a ring on our finger. In part, because it leads neatly to nuclear families. And nuclear families are lucrative. They squeeze people into the smallest units possible: each family buys a house, car, and television. The more family units, the more houses, cars, and televisions get purchased. Goods are duplicated and sold, instead of shared, so more profit is generated.

The idea that love is exclusive to romantic partners, however, skews our understanding of love. It isolates us and makes us vulnerable to bad loving. Tightening love to romantic edges reduces our sample size, and if love is defined by a few people, as opposed to the average of many, love becomes lopsided. We have nothing to compare bad love to, so we normalize poor loving: romantic partnerships and their subsequent nuclear families are where women are most likely to experience violence, discrimination, and unequal distribution of household labor.[2]

"They say it is love," writes feminist Silvia Federici. "We say it is unwaged work."[3]

It does not have to be this way. Love was never uniquely the permanent, exclusive terrain of romantic partners and nuclear families. It takes a village to be loved. Nearly half of enslaved Black people were severed from romantic partners and parents, relying on broader collectivity for love instead.[4] Many Indigenous cultures practice more expansive notions of kinship, too, like the Lenni Lenape people's matrilocal families. Nuclear families are not ubiquitously bad—for communities of color in the US, they have also been sites of refuge and resistance—but they are often inadequate. They are not organic, biological molds to shepherd all our love into. They only seem that way. Love might appear intangible—as real and absolute as air—but love is also an ideology, something we learn.

Insisting that love is finite, experienced only through blood or marriage, makes us believe love is scarce. If something is scarce, we value it more. If love is advertised as it really is—free, abundant—people will not pay a price for it. People will not subjugate themselves to bad love, if they know there is something better.

In 1991, anthropologist Kath Weston coined the term "chosen families," practiced in queer communities. When so many queer, trans, and gender-diverse people are rejected, friends become family. Families reveal a conditional kind of care, but chosen families glisten in a promise of unconditional care. Not unconditional because anything is tolerated, but unconditional because you are accepted for who you are. Chosen families build a kinship that is supple, based on choice, not blood.[5]

I know of two friends who became the custodial guardians of a child together. The child's mother was incarcerated during a protest. Sitting in a bank, requesting a loan to buy a house for their new family, the bank manager blinked at the friends.

"You're not married?" he asked. "You're not romantically involved at all?"

Biological families are like lotteries.[6] You cannot choose them, so love becomes condemned to your circumstances. This punctuates inequity: relying on family inheritance for love does not work if your family has none to give. Chosen families, however, are a social reordering toward friends. A loving of friends, a loyalty to them, a consideration of them as your family by choice. Anyone can practice this; whether abandoned because of your gender, sexuality, unconventional career, or political values, you do not have to accept your circumstances. Friendsmases and Friendsgivings can move from supplementary celebrations to central ones. From side dishes to main dishes. Friendship can cast your nets wider, beyond your circumstances.

The summer of 1966, June Jordan's husband left for graduate school and never came back. In her essay, "Many Rivers to Cross," June describes moving back into her parents' home with her eight-year-old son. Her father discarded her as a failure. She was pregnant again, despite having had three illegal, expensive abortions. She tried making cash fast, but she could not bend, carry heavy items, walk, or sit straight without vomiting and "acute abdominal pain."

Late one night, there was a knock at June's bedroom door. Rubbing her eyes, June opened it. Standing there was her father, wearing an odd expression. He said it was something about her mother.

"I think she's dead, but I'm not sure," he said, avoiding June's eyes.

"What do you mean?"

"I want you to go downstairs and figure it out."

June said, "You want me to figure out if my mother is dead or alive?"

June did. She yelled for help. Her mom had committed suicide.

It only got worse: June started bleeding heavily, so she was rushed to the hospital.

"As a mother without a husband, as a poet without a publisher, a freelance journalist without assignment, a city planner without contract," June writes, she felt her situation "had suddenly eliminated the whole realm of choice from my life."

Choice, a way out and forward, was returned to June through friendship, through her family of choice. Hitting rock bottom, it was not her husband or parents who aided her. Her aunts and cousin supported her, but, passionately, her friends did too.

Upon realizing her mom was dead, June had run to the

telephone and called a friend, "a woman who talked back loud to me so that I could realize my growing hysteria and check it."

Later, at Harlem Hospital, where June was admitted for bleeding, she woke up and grew frantic. Where was her son? Where was Christopher? Her cousin calmed her. June's friends were "taking turns with him."[7]

Friendship puts into question everything we take for granted. Love is not buried within marriage and families. We can have romantic soulmates and platonic ones. We can have nuclear families and chosen ones. Love does not have one mold. Love should not have limits. It should not have conditions.

The Survey Center for American Life reports Americans are "now more likely to make friends at work than any other way—including at school, in their neighborhood, at their place of worship, or even through existing friends."[8]

Seeing corporate workplaces as your "fampany," as one tech company calls itself (consider, too, popular terms like "work husband" and "work wife"), means accepting a limited version of love as well. One that is conditional on your productivity and profitability, not *un*conditional, as it should be. As journalist Sarah Jaffe observed in *Work Won't Love You Back*, a consequence of "fampanies" is the replacement of real community with work community. And if we turn to work to replace "the love we lack elsewhere," it will hurt, because the love workplaces show is inherently shallow and stipulatory.[9]

When June was fighting breast cancer, the University of California, Berkeley refused to give her medical leave from teaching, despite June's continued requests right until her death.[10] It was not her workplace that loved her, but her friends who traveled from around the world to nurse her alongside her primary partner. Friendship is powerful because it is untethered by institutions like marriage, nuclear families, and corporations, which prioritize profit, even if you are the cost.

We have one word—"love"—that covers the thousands of feelings you will experience throughout your life. In ancient Greece, love was known by three different words, each specifying a special kind of love. Broadly, "agape" was a love for something bigger than you, like a community or God. "Philia" was love for friends and other nonsexual relations, like your family. And "eros" was love for sexual partners.[11]

Today, love singularly means eros, not philia or agape. When we think of falling in love, and love at first sight, and the most significant utterances of "I love you" in our lives, we think of romantic partners, or people we are sexually and romantically involved with. But if we define love, drawing a box around it, we will have trouble feeling it, because so much of the love we experience falls outside that box. Love is agape, philia, eros, and everything in between and beyond. We know it when we feel it. And when we feel it, we can use it to guide us. Whether love flutters into our chest from a poem, a baby's laugh, a warm breeze, or from a friend's company, we can remember its texture, and we can use it as a standard, as writer and Black feminist Audre Lorde says, "an internal sense of satisfaction to which, once we have experienced it, we know we can aspire."[12]

We are taught to believe that blood is thicker than water, but we should loosen that concept. Anyway, it is a misquote. The original is "blood of the covenant is thicker than water of the womb." Covenant, at the time, meant the bonds you chose, not the bonds you were born into via "the womb." Meaning, the untruncated version actually celebrates chosen ties, not blood ones.[13]

And why not? I experience love in my friendships. My standards for love are unconstrained because my friendships grow a love without ceilings. Bad love is not normalized in my friendships. When living with my friends, responsibilities are shared, transcending gender roles, preventing me from lowering my standards in especially heteronormative romantic partnerships. Good friendship can acquaint us with good love, shielding us from tolerating anything less.

bell hooks writes, "Many of us learn as children that friendship should never be seen as just as important as family ties. However, friendship is the place in which a great majority of us have our first glimpse of redemptive love and caring community. Learning to love in friendships empowers us in ways that enable us to bring this love to other interactions with family or with romantic bonds."[14]

We can raise our standards of love through the bonds of friendship. First, we unlearn that romantic love is the epitome of happiness, that love begins when we get married, as the movies suggest. If you rush to that destination, you will miss a million miles of love. Love is now. Love is abundant, fulfilling, and brilliant among friends too.

We also understand that true love makes you courageous. To step away from bad love, to demand more, to be fiercer about what kind of loving you deserve: one that is good, one that is just. One that does not seem scarce.

Practicing love like this, you not only become kinder to yourself and your friends, you also become kinder to your romantic partner(s) and biological or legal family.

Almost 50 percent of marriages end in divorce or separation.[15] Perhaps because, in the end, we go looking for too much in one person. A romantic partner cannot be your everything. As humans, we need many connections.

Expecting all social needs to be met by one person is unfair and unkind pressure to put on them. It sets romantic relationships up for failure.

Seeing love as exclusive to your family is unfair as well. The exhaustion and self-sacrifices of parenthood, of sleepless nights with wailing babies, is romanticized as a rite of passage of sorts. But as the daughter of immigrants, I want to lighten the load off my parents' shoulders. Why must my dreams always come at the expense of theirs?

Expanding our imaginations beyond the nuclear household as the source for love and care might seem improbable, but it is not. You probably have already experienced it. Looking back, who would you be giving long-overdue credit to? Whose faces appear? Those people who mothered and fathered you, despite not being your biological mother and father. Those people who hugged you close, who loved you like a romantic partner, without necessarily being one.

We should see love not as an identity—a spouse, parent, or child—but as a discipline.

Love is not scarce, absurd, or unattainable. Love shimmers in our friendships.

Friendship is the great love story we have been looking for.

10.

Friends Learn Together

IN ONE INSTALLMENT of the Harry Potter books, the Ministry of Magic appoints Dolores Umbridge as professor of the Dark Arts. With this government intervention, the Hogwarts School of Witchcraft and Wizardry becomes a surveillance state. Student activity is restricted, disciplinary punishments escalate, and the curricula spouts Ministry propaganda instead of skills for surviving in the Wizarding world.

In protest, the students summon the Room of Requirement. If you walk by the Room of Requirement three times reciting what you require, the room reveals itself, equipped with your needs. So the students fashion it into their own school, learning spells in the dimly lit cavernous space into which the Room of Requirement transforms. On metallic dummies, they learn the Expelliarmus charm for disarming opponents, and Stupefy for stunning them. They help one another learn Patronus, an advanced spell for repelling Dementors, the deathly creatures with black cloaks, skeleton fingers, and yawning mouths that suck souls from bodies.

The series' protagonists, Harry, Ron, and Hermione, show a friendship capable of destroying oppressive regimes and villainous tyrants. I am aware that this rare example is even more rare because all three, Harry, Ron, and Hermione, are fictitious. Regardless, there are parallels between our friendships today and these magical friends. Our schooling has also silenced the education that we require. Our friendships can also become our Rooms of Requirement.

Conversations between friends outside of institutions— across dinner tables, in coffee shops, during walks, while grabbing lunch, or on the subway—are where so much education occurs. In *The Undercommons: Fugitive Planning & Black Study*, Fred Moten and Stefano Harney describe this phenomenon as "study," a "common intellectual practice" that may stray from what we are accustomed to, like textbooks, universities, and the learning that occurs within institutional walls.

Instead, Moten says, "I think we are committed to the

idea that study is what you do with other people. It's talking and walking around with other people, working, dancing, suffering, some irreducible convergence of all three, held under the name of speculative practice."[1]

It makes sense for friends to engage in "study," as Moten describes, beyond institutions. You cannot learn everything from traditional sources, because traditional sources are absent of so many perspectives.

Anti-literacy laws inhibited enslaved and free Black people from learning how to read and write. For Indigenous peoples, their own languages were prohibited. Many communities of color preserved their histories through storytelling and oral traditions. Yet, oral histories, compared to written primary sources, are not commonly valued as "hard knowledge" in academia. What we consider knowledge itself is limited.

"All of us in this country have been educated by white people who have been educated by white people who have been educated by white people...that's the paradigm we're fighting," the author Anika Nailah once told me, one chilly Vermont afternoon.

A creative solution—friendship—bursts from these constraints. We learn, and remember, among one another instead.

It was late at night as I watched my parents serve chai

so hot the milk curdled. Under the kitchen table's orange light, hands gripped around steaming cups, they sat with friends. The cliché is that immigrants are torn between two worlds. But through loud discussion, shifting between English, Hindi, and Telugu, my parents and their friends discussed how the India they knew was long gone. Skyscrapers erupted over farmland. While they used to trek miles for a Popsicle, now, motorcycles arrive at people's doorsteps, ice cream wedged inside dried ice, vapor billowing out of the plastic bag. They talked, and continued talking until an innocent, shy topic gained more force, more vigor, more sharpness, and, like a sculptor working her knife through thick clay, finally revealed a legible thought: their situation is more tragic than simply being stuck between two countries. They are stuck between their new country and a country that no longer exists, except in their memories.

Friendship can be the most valuable site of "study" in your life, the most prominent site of learning, repurposed for rebellious convening. You and your friends craft your own curricula. You affirm what your formal education did not. You make relevant what it neglected. You examine the events of your lives and connect them to one another's realities. You hammer at what is supposedly insignificant, forging it into significance. You expand your visions, acknowledging that an "incessant and irreversible intellectuality of these activities," as Moten says, was already there, in the fabric of your very lives.[2] Together, you workshop new possibilities. Friendship makes artists of us all, creating something out of nothing, and this creative power is cataclysmic.

"Artists together with creative persons of all sorts," writes Rollo May in *The Courage to Create*, "are the possible destroyers of our nicely ordered systems."[3]

In one photo I love, members of the Combahee River Collective are squeezed together, arms around shoulders, some smiling, others serious, one wearing blue, holding a Black doll, another wearing white. They look young, these friends. Together they created the monumental radical Black feminist theory of the seventies and eighties, crafting much of what we understand today as "intersectionality."

As an antidote to atomization, they would gather for several days, typically in someone's borrowed house.

One of the Combahee's founders Barbara Smith said, "It was to have serious political discussion. It was to have cultural and social opportunities and outlets. It was everything. It was multipurpose, three days of everything... There was food of a level you could not even imagine. Because my sister and I, we loved to cook. Demita is one of the best cooks on the planet. So we would throw down."[4]

In Harry Potter, the Room of Requirement materializes out of thin air, with all the necessary resources to plug the gaps in Harry, Ron, and Hermione's knowledge. In real life, a room for friends to interchange knowledge may not appear magically. You must put time and energy into finding ways to connect, thinking outside of every box. Like the Combahee, sometimes you travel thousands of miles to convene, even if for a few days. Other times, if you look carefully, you will find the Room of Requirement opens up right where you are.

Once together, friends talk in circles, write in each other's notebooks, cook, laugh, and exchange stories and resources. Such friendship is how you grow your consciousness, examine your identities, heartbreaks, and longings, how you begin to consider your stances on wars and politics.

"I'm not saying that there were no kinds of tensions among and between us," Barbara clarified.[5] But tension within your Room of Requirement starts to feel routine, expected even, because you are uninspired by airtight ideas. With one another, you would rather push your thoughts into the turbulent, windy skies of expansion and practice. Because learning cannot happen in isolation; ideas need to be tossed around and whittled. Good friends help to toughen, complicate, and ground our own thinking.[6] Without experimentation and exposure, like a newborn, ideas will not develop the immunity needed to survive.

Friendship makes you courageous enough to believe in your ideas as well. Exiting your Room of Requirement, your friends become a mental safeguard.

"Women have to do impossible things and think impossible thoughts," writes feminist philosopher Marilyn Frye. "Without a community...an individual cannot keep hold of her radical insights..."[7]

Even if you are not a woman, but an independent thinker marginalized for another reason, friendship becomes the community through which you hold on to your radical insights.

Researching June Jordan's archived letters at Harvard's Schlesinger Library, I went through boxes of letters between June and her friends, many of whom were in the same field, struggling for jobs, credibility, income, and recognition. In their correspondences, June edited friends' manuscripts and asked for feedback on her own. Expressing urgency about finishing a project and needing a place to stay, her friends wrote back, saying to stay at theirs. These friends shared their highest highs and lowest lows, trusting each other with such tender information, refusing to let anyone fall behind. They were responsible and gentle with one another, knowing that vulnerabilities are better protected by two sets of hands, as opposed to one.

Most of us do not see friends as collaborators. We

separate ourselves and our work from friends instead, envisioning them as competitors.

A college professor of mine once leaned over his desk and said, "Stop starting sentences with 'My friends and I.' Build your own name! Launch your own career! Claim your own ideas!"

We are taught to share toys with friends as kids, but, as adults, to be selfish and suspicious. Friends become rulers. Standing beside them, we measure how far ahead or behind we are in life. We rarely drop our guard. We may even expect friends to screw us over, to leverage personal information against us or for themselves, especially if we think the relationship will inevitably end or drift.

But friendship does not have to match the plot of *The Social Network*.

In 1977, June and her friend Alice Walker, author of *The Color Purple*, arranged a get-together in June's New York City apartment. They called it the Sisterhood.

In a photograph of the Sisterhood's first meeting, writers and artists Vertamae Smart-Grosvenor, Lori Sharpe, Nana Maynard, Ntozake Shange, Audreen Ballard, Alice Walker, and Toni Morrison all smile at the camera in their heavy winter coats. Next to Toni, June leans against a wall, hands crossed behind her back, grinning especially large.[8]

Alice said, "Well, The Sisterhood was the brainchild of

myself and June Jordan... We would not let the establishment put one of us ahead of the other."[9]

Putting "one of us ahead of the other," as Alice said, only helps "the establishment," which benefits from us fighting each other, instead of fighting it. In reality, we need one another.

Stirring orchestras play in the movies as someone, standing alone facing a blackboard, brow furrowed, index finger pressed to his lip, exclaims that he has cracked a code. But knowledge is not a stubborn entity dropped from the heavens, knowledge is a continuous, collaborative process. Knowledge is iterative. It does not materialize from an abyss, but intensifies like lightning branching and forking from people's combined brainpower. It is a collaboration so intricate that trying to identify an idea's origin becomes convoluted, like trying to reverse engineer a soup's recipe. Was it the broth that added the flavor, the star anise, or the cooking temperature? Realistically, it was everything, everybody.

This changes how we understand learning. Knowledge does not get delivered; it is not something you sit passively at a desk and receive. You cannot be stingy with your ideas; you must commune for them to gain force. We must collaborate, not compete.

This was once a more normal concept. Our association

of "academy" with "education" originates from Plato's Academy, circa 387 BCE, where Plato created the first Western university on the land of a man named Academus.[10] The Academy was built around collaboration. The lore is that Aristotle, Plato's student, and others would roam through the halls, discussing and challenging one another. In fact, for Plato, "philosophy" meant friendship: philosophy is derived from the ancient Greek "philos," meaning love, which is also connected to "philia," the word for friendship.[11] Plato considered philosophy the act of "reasoning together."[12] And although these men imagined philosophy as only available to the elite educated ruling class, friendship can be an intellectual space for us, too.

Friendship is how knowledge is formed. You begin enjoying not only the end result, the lightbulb moment, the idea itself, but its creation process. You embrace a disposition. As you lean into creativity, you lean into community too. Ideas bring us closer to people we never could have imagined being friends with. Like the architects who collaborated with scientists to incorporate a sharkskin pattern into hospital doorknobs, because bacteria attach less to it.[13]

Friendship is a renegade educational space. Everything changes when you recognize study as this, occurring between friends. You may never remember that letter grade from college, but you will remember that 3:00 am conversation with your roommate. It legitimizes that joke about women traveling to bathrooms together in order to exchange thoughts; it is not frivolous, unserious behavior, but an equally important moment of intellectuality and connection, even if forced to the fringes.

"That recognition," Fred Moten says, "allows you to access a whole, varied, alternative history of thought."[14]

11.

A Friend Named Mentor

IN THE ANCIENT Greek epic poem the *Odyssey*, King Odysseus leaves his son Telemachus to fight in the Trojan war for twenty years. He asks his friend, a man named Mentor, to guide Telemachus while he is gone. The goddess of wisdom Athena transforms into Mentor, becoming the literal embodiment of wisdom to advise Odysseus's son instead. Athena's intent, she explains to the gods on Mount Olympus, is to put "menos" into Telemachus. "Menos" means mental fortitude.[1]

Mentorship is often just another name for intergenerational friendship. But the word "mentorship," rather than "friendship," is stifling. Like Athena, mentors must be divine, superior, and all-knowing, offering menos to the young. In reaction, mentees must perform indebted and inferior.

"Intergenerational friendship" gives age-bridging bonds a better chance at sticking. In a 2022 study, nearly 43 percent of American respondents said they have not "spoken seriously in the past year" with different generations outside their families.[2] Although the US was the most age-integrated society in the beginning of the twentieth century, today, it is among the most age-segregated. Research suggests younger and older people "are the most isolated groups in society."[3]

Mentorship casts out a superiority-inferiority template we must squeeze inside in order to connect intergenerationally. It is framed as "mono-directional," as writer Steven Strott says, with mentors giving wisdom or menos to their mentees, which exacerbates power dynamics between ages.[4] Intergenerational friendship, however, insists that someone's superiority does not need to gain legibility by contrasting your inferiority. You can be someone's student, but still their equal. We see that older people carry wisdom, and younger people do too. Wisdom is dialogical, produced from a tension between experience and intuition, between the well-trained eye and the fresh one. It is an important balance. My older friends remind me of how much better things are now compared to how they were, but I remind them of how much better things still can be.

Reconfiguring intergenerational bonds as friendship,

younger friends are not talked down to by older friends, who assume their inexperience. Older friends are not dehumanized and shamed by younger friends, who presume they are "just old." We stop restricting intergenerational bonds to formal, professional roles and welcome day-to-day interactions, learning, and challenges like we would with any friend.[5] Day-to-day association scrubs the celebrity complex from mentors, humanizing them, exposing their imperfections. This might violate what we imagine an older person is—goddess-like—but it brings us refreshingly closer to what a good friend is.

Not every mentorship is an intergenerational friendship, just as every relationship is not a friendship. Intergenerational friendships might require distance. Boundaries are necessary even because of the power dynamics between older and younger people, especially keeping in mind grooming's prevalence, or when older people befriend younger people in order to abuse or exploit them.[6] But sometimes mentorship is its own kind of friendship in disguise. Sometimes allowing that one relationship you automatically categorized as a mentorship, simply because of age, the grace to be more like a friendship introduces reciprocity into your bond that resurrects it.

R. Buckminster Fuller was June's friend, but their relationship began as a stiff mentor-mentee one: Mr. Fuller was an architect forty-one years older than June. He wore suits with pocket squares and stylish black horn-rimmed glasses. He was white, attended Harvard University, and won the Presidential Medal of Freedom in 1983.

When June met him, her husband had just abandoned her and her son. She was broke.

"A few friends," she writes, "bought me cigarettes, Scotch, eggs, bread, and my mother gave me two or three dollars for gas money."

For an *Esquire* magazine writing assignment, June proposed a project with Mr. Fuller, whom she did not know. She hoped to collaborate "on an architectural redesign of Harlem."[7]

Architecture, like writing and poetry, shapes how we feel and move through spaces. The way a building welcomes in light can relieve you like a good sonnet can. Realizing this, June would take the bus from Queens to a public library on Fifty-Third Street in Manhattan, educating herself on architects, particularly on Mr. Fuller. She wanted to design better public housing for Harlem's majority Black residents. It was a risk. She knew that. She wrote to Mr. Fuller nevertheless and waited.[8]

"I put my whole life on the line: Now I would work and work and work and wait on this beginning, as a writer, thinker, poet."[9]

Mr. Fuller wrote back.

June began calling him Bucky. Their collaboration was colorful, alive from their minds' unconventional pairing, thrumming with mutual, overflowing respect. Their relationship was lasting and meaningful, not quick and rigid like a mentorship, because Bucky never presented himself as godlike, like Athena. He made his failures known. He attended Harvard but never graduated; he was expelled twice, once for skipping midterm exams and being too social.[10] His daughter died at three years old from spinal meningitis, and, reeling from the loss, with no job or savings, when Bucky was around thirty years old, he stood at Lake Michigan's edge, preparing to drown himself until a thought stalled him.

It urged him to live, to apply himself "to converting all [his] experience to the highest advantage of others."[11]

Bucky stepped away from Lake Michigan.

Most of us move in self-segregated packs. We are Boomers, Gen X, Millennials, Gen Z, Gen Alpha, and so on. We move in circles with friends who look and sound like us, who know the same music and were brought up under the same presidents. Without good friendships with other generations, how can we picture anything else? Different vantage points though, for both the elderly and the young, offer important friction to the confirmation biases we insulate ourselves within.

Without intergenerational friendship, June Jordan

would not have become who she became. Neither would have others, like Dr. Martin Luther King Jr. When Martin was around twenty-six years old, E. D. Nixon, organizer of the Montgomery Bus Boycott, asked for his help with the movement. Unsure, because he was young and new in town, Martin asked for some time to think. Nixon said sure, and he made some other phone calls. When he called Martin back, Martin said all right.

"I'm glad of that Reverend King," Nixon said. "Cause I talked to eighteen other people. I told them to meet at your church at three o'clock this evening."[12]

Thirty years older than Martin, Nixon propelled a local activist and preacher into a globally renowned organizer who helped one of the greatest boycotts in American history. Older friends see in you what even you do not see in yourself.

Especially through this political lens, rather than seeing intergenerational bonds as one-sided, we see their reciprocity, which qualifies them for a term like friendship: you see that while younger friends might not give back now, the promise of giving later is enough. Prestige and fame often get confused with impact, but we should disassociate the two. Although younger friends might not be able to give money, contacts, recommendations, etcetera, they can give something back to the world, in terms of the actions they take to carry the work forward.

If Bucky's purpose, as he realized standing by Lake Michigan, was to better the lives of others, younger friendships assist. We are not here long. We cannot accomplish everything alone. Older friends share their friendship not based on your performance, but your promise. Not for prestige, how flashy you can make their network, or for the favors you will owe them, but because of what you can *do*. With faith in how you will carry their legacy forward through what you might do next.

As we unhook mentorship from age, opportunities swell: now, good friends—even if our own age—can be conceptualized as mentors. Traditional mentors require privilege and luck. Not everyone has access to direct ancestors, including the descendants of the enslaved, refugees, and other migrants, to call on for some guidance. Not everyone has a Dumbledore or Gandalf figure to pick them from a crowd and lead them forward either.

Age cannot dictate who is a mentor. All of our friends are mentors, regardless of their age. Aristotle believed friends are mirrors, but I think they are more.[13] They see not only what is there, like mirrors, but guide you into becoming the better version of yourself just around the corner.

I internalize many demeaning ideas about myself, which my friends mentor me out of. I thought I could not run, but

Ariana and Châu encouraged me to watch my breathing, slowing their paces to run by my side, helping me find good shoes, then, as my distances increased, to hone my mental focus, plan my routes, and eventually sign up for races. I thought I was a bad driver, because of gender stereotypes in my family that made me nervous to even drive down the street, but then Nastasia pushed me to drive with her in Europe, on narrow mountain paths on the opposite side of the road. As we returned our rental car, she smiled and leaned her head back against the headrest. There was pride in her eyes. She had known I could do it, even though I had not.

As the French-born essayist Anaïs Nin wrote, "Each friend represents in us, a world possibly not born until they arrive, and it is only by this meeting that a new world is born."

My favorite example of this is between writers Maya Angelou and James Baldwin. Maya's book, *I Know Why the Caged Bird Sings* changed lives, pushed the possibilities of self-expression, particularly Black self-expression, was nominated for the National Book Award, and, as of 2020, sold over two million copies since its publication in 1969.[14] But she would not have written it without her friend, James Baldwin.

Dr. Martin Luther King Jr. was assassinated on April 4, 1968; April fourth was Maya's birthday, and Martin was Maya's friend.

"I had been planning a birthday party," Maya said. "I had planned to join [Martin] after my birthday. [His death] shocked me so that I stopped eating, I refused to answer the phone."

James came to Maya's apartment. She remembers him shouting, "Open this door! Open this door!" He was cursing, making a ruckus, refusing to leave "until the police came."

Maya relented. She opened the door, and James flooded in.

"Go and have a bath. I'll wait and I'll have some clothes for you."

He pulled clothes from Maya's closet. He said, "I'm taking you someplace."

Maya recalls, "Now I had no idea where he was taking me, but he had a car outside the driveway. We went to another house, a brownstone not too far from where I lived. When we got into the house he introduced me to Jules Feiffer and Jules's wife at the time, Judy, and their daughter. Jules said, 'You need to laugh, and you need to have somebody watch you laugh and laugh with you.' In that sparkling company, I did come out of myself."[15]

They talked until three or four in the morning, sipping on scotch. Maya's stories animated the room. She was born in St. Louis, Missouri, and became a mother at age seventeen. Eventually, she moved to New York to become a dancer, working unexpectedly as a composer, singer, actor, journalist, and educator. In 1960, she fell in love with a South African freedom fighter, married him, resigned from the Southern Christian Leadership Conference, where she had met Martin, and moved to Cairo, Egypt, becoming editor of the *Arab Observer*. When her marriage ended, she lived in Ghana with her son, only returning to the US in 1966.[16]

After listening to Maya speak during that dinner on April fourth, the dinner James dragged Maya to in order to distract her from her grief, Judy, one of the hosts, called a friend at a publishing company.

She said, "You know the poet Maya Angelou? If you could get her to write a book…"[17]

James was only four years older than Maya, but friends like James, even if your own age, are mentors too. Because all good friends reach into you and pull out who they know you can be. You might not know you are smart, until a friend tells you. You might not know you are funny, until a friend tells you. We are like water, filling whatever container our friends shape for us. The world is as wide or as narrow as the people we surround ourselves with, as my professor Ruha Benjamin advised me. If your friend's vision for you is small, limiting, demeaning, then you contain yourself within those limits. Good friends like James, however, toss aside containers and encourage you to be creative.

In her eulogy for James, Toni Morrison said, "Like many of us left here I thought I knew you. Now I discover that in your company it is myself I know. That is the astonishing gift of your art and your friendship: You gave us ourselves to think about, to cherish."[18]

Laura Flanders, someone close to June Jordan, said something similar of June: "[June] wrote of [Dr. Martin Luther King Jr.] that because he taught us the value of our lives, we have become capable of saving them. And that's what June did. She taught each of us, individually, those of us who knew her, the value of our lives. She believed so adamantly in our worth that eventually we had to take ourselves as seriously as she did."[19]

All good friends, regardless of age, are mentors in this way. All good friends have Athena, the goddess of wisdom, flickering inside them. Coaching us into ourselves, banging on our door when we feel hopeless and small, shouting for us to cherish ourselves, to remember the value of our lives, so that we become capable of saving them.

An editor named Robert Loomis reached out to Maya, asking her to write about her life.

She said no.

James stepped in one more time. "If you want Maya

Angelou to do something," he told Robert, "tell her she can't do it."[20]

Robert remarked to Maya that an autobiography could not be good literature.

"I will start tomorrow," was Maya's response, and, during that dark time, some light finally glimmered. She started writing *I Know Why the Caged Bird Sings*.[21]

12.

The Unremitting Friend

DR. M. SHADEE MALAKLOU was offered a job at Berea College in Kentucky in 2019. She stood in front of Dr. bell hooks, a faculty member at Berea, with flowers she "could not afford."[1]

bell nodded her head at Dr. Malaklou and winked. "I was against your hire," she said.[2]

"That was bell," Dr. Malaklou told me. "She didn't switch on and off in terms of polite society and code switching. She didn't do that."

bell was hesitant about Dr. Malaklou's hire, because she thought the city of Berea would be lonely for an Iranian American like her. She could have said nothing—most of us prefer flattery and exaggerated praise in our friendships—but bell's first words to Dr. Malaklou were truthful, establishing a precedent, and setting into motion a good friendship.

Scholar John Felstiner says, "Nouns normally serve to identify things in space, verbs to release them in time."[3]

Friendship (noun) identifies the relation. Truth-telling (verb) releases it.

Over the next three years of bell's life, bell and Dr. Malaklou became good friends. Dr. Malaklou would order towers of Juicy Fruit gum for bell and bring bell her groceries; bell would call Dr. Malaklou to eat Indian food and grab cheeseburgers.[4] Dr. Malaklou, along with bell's sister, was among the few people bell saw before she died.

bell practiced a particular feminism rooted, in bell's words, in "the cultural ethos of the Kentucky backwoods, of the hillbilly country folk who were my ancestors and kin."[5] A rugged frankness matching Kentucky's own country terrain. Calling you out, Dr. Malaklou writes in one article, so that you could be called in and into an unshakable structure of truthful, unremitting friendship.[6]

Being honest does not mean spilling your guts, or disrespecting privacy.

In *All About Love: New Visions* bell says, "We all need spaces where we can be alone with thoughts and feelings—where we can experience healthy psychological autonomy and can choose to share when we want to."

Being honest does mean, however, acknowledging that there is a difference between privacy and secrets.[7]

Secrets are usually lies. You lie to control a situation in your favor—to receive extra attention by exaggerating accomplishments, to prevent blowback by minimizing wrongdoings. Lying is a form of manipulation, and a bond leashed by manipulation is not a true bond. There is a difference between a caged bird, and a bird that flies freely to and from your window. Avoiding honesty keeps friendships imprisoned. With you, but under false pretenses. Evasion dispossesses friendships the chance to depart from peripheral relationships into important, reliable ones. Ones that do not need cages to stay.

In a 2002 letter to an unnamed friend, whom we will call John, June Jordan says, "I am choked with horror."

John's classmate Danny was abducted and murdered in Pakistan. Danny was an international activist. He enjoyed building relationships with "people entirely different from himself," like with a Pakistani Islamist and the son of a Holocaust survivor.

John found out about Danny's death in the newspaper.

Gently, June asked John how he was doing, and John said, "I'm furious! And I wanted somebody to deal with this fact: Danny was killed because he was a Jew!...what can we/what should we—as a community/a community of Jews—what should we do?"

Touching his shoulder as he made his way to the door,
June had few words. So she wrote him the letter. She was
not in his Jewish community, but she wanted "to figure out
a way to stand beside [them,] and a way to stand together."

Do not forget context, June urged. While mourning
Danny, do not forget his hope for peace. Do not forget
how Israeli soldiers killed twenty-four-year-old Issa Faraj
in the West Bank Dheisheh refugee camp, Israeli tanks
attacked journalists near the al-Amari refugee camp, and
thirty-eight Palestinians were killed by Israeli troops in
Ramallah. In other words, two things could be true at the
same time. John's friend was gone, and that was devastating, but it should not eclipse the fuller story.

June asked, "Can we stand face-to-face, and tell the
truth to each other?"

"I can't even undertake to write to you / to reach
out to you, my friend, without the unholy carnage of
Israel-Palestine exploding in my face... If I can trust you,
still, to hear my grief for Danny, and to share my grief
for Issa Faraj—If we refuse double standards churning to
deform friends into enemies—Oh!"

Reading June's letter, I felt nervous. Danny—John's
friend—was dead, and June did not dampen her frankness
in her letter to John, even amid John's grief. I felt nervous,
too, listening to Dr. Malaklou describe bell's honesty. bell

never seemed to curb her honesty either. Was this the time for such honesty?

June writes, "Your Danny is dead. And how can we honor his heroic wish: 'to change the world?' I have no simple answers. But perhaps our willingness to listen and to say all that we know, and feel—all that we dare—perhaps that will help us to build something better than we can even, now, imagine."[8]

I had no reason to be nervous. Honesty flexes a friendship's strength. Dishonesty signals weak friendship. Honesty is how friendship grows deep. How it becomes real. Every instance your friendship survives an honest conversation, a realization about the nature of your bond sinks in: you both could have kept silent—societally, there are few strings binding you—but you did not. Taking the risk and being honest even when uneasy, even when unobligated, reveals your respect for and trust in each other. While there is no standard recipe for honesty, no right way to be honest, there is an underlying principle distinguishing good friendships: respecting friends enough to try anyway.

Most people prefer pleasant friendships, keeping things comfortable, rather than good. We should not confuse the two, though. There is a difference between pleasantness and goodness. Goodness requires honesty, even if unpleasant. Pleasantness requires maintaining pleasantness, even if it is dishonest. Between pleasantness and goodness, friends should strive for goodness, that is how you demarcate the relationship of a good friend. This is why a good friend looks like bell, winking at Dr. Malaklou on her doorstep, or June, penning that letter to John. A relationship not always pleasant, but good. A relationship not always breezy, but also not superficial. Rather, it is trusting and muscular.

Friendship can be both good and pleasant, too.

James Baldwin writes about his friend Lorraine Hansberry, "We spent a lot of time arguing about history and tremendously related subjects in her Bleecker Street and, later, Waverly Place flats. And often, just when I was certain that she was about to throw me out as being altogether too rowdy a type, she would stand up, her hands on her hips (for these down-home sessions she always wore slacks), and pick up my empty glass as though she intended to throw it at me. Then she would walk into the kitchen, saying, with a haughty toss of her head, 'Really, Jimmy. You ain't right, child!' With which stern put-down she would hand me another drink and launch into a brilliant analysis of just why I wasn't 'right.'"

Pleasantness is not always a cost of goodness. After those heated nights, dizzied by their friendship's transparency, that sense of holding nothing back, James writes, "I would often stagger down her stairs as the sun came up, usually in the middle of a paragraph and always in the middle of a laugh. That marvelous laugh. That marvelous face. I loved her, she was my sister and my comrade."[9]

Honesty does not always mean pivotal high-stakes conversations. Honesty also means ordinary, daily transparency. Arriving as your raw self to friendships. Admitting when you are tired, mistaken, impatient, or sad, even if you are clumsy while doing it, even if you have not wrestled profound insight from your suffering to reward the friends who listen. Honesty means trusting friends to welcome you as you are, absent of performance. This brings you closer. Your raw, unmasked selves can touch more unhindered. Being honest is important because in doing so we greet "our own complexity," as Adrienne Rich writes.[10] Honesty is how you love friends deeper and truer.

If you feel incapable of honesty within a friendship, your bond is likely superficial and wobbly. Most of us are overly hesitant to be honest, revealed by "frienderventions"—when friends gather to vocalize honesty about another friend's behavior. Frienderventions are multiple friends confronting one person. They are ceremonious when they should be unexceptional. We seem to know that multiple friends are required, for strength in numbers, to feel audacious enough for honesty.

You can try, as June Jordan calls it, the "acrobatics of

self-denial" in favor of the superficial ease of avoiding the elephant in the room, also "for the sake of those real and enormous areas of mutual agreement."[11] But evasion is never sustainable. Withholding honesty begins to splinter friendship's foundation.

Good friends are intimate thought partners dwelling inside your mental world. You see a friend's favorite snack, and you buy it. You hear a song reminding you of her, and you text her. You mull over an epiphany of hers for weeks, amazed by her genius. With honest communication, a clear bridge materializes between your brains. It is a strongly felt intimacy.

If you always bite your tongue, however—saying, "that didn't hurt my feelings," because you are too impassive to say otherwise; or, "what you did to him wasn't mean, he totally deserved it," even if he did not, but you are worried your honesty could backfire on you—an object settles between you on that bridge. That mental intimacy gets tainted, blocked. To clear it, to pursue a friendship of integrity without guilt or reservation, we should speak candidly. When confused, hurt, or let down, we should talk, and we should trust each other to listen. In other words, we should trust in the friendship.

We are taught to lie to please and appease others so exhaustively that we become strangers to ourselves, unsure of our own true feelings, which causes "depression and loss of self-awareness," as bell observes.[12]

Dishonesty, swallowing your own discomfort for the convenience of others, becomes a definitive experience. Especially for women, who are portrayed as inherently *un*trustworthy, tracing back Adam and Eve and that apple.[13] This self-silencing gets compounded based on your background and personal history. You owe it to yourself to be honest, to not shoulder your honest truths alone. To say that you are, in fact, too tired to join today. To voice how, *actually*, what he said did hurt your feelings.

Without honesty, friends are not mirrors, as Aristotle wanted, friends are carnival mirrors that distort our foreheads and chins, dizzying us.

Lying culture has political consequences. It makes people less courageous. Lying and fear go hand in hand, just as honesty and courage do. By building honesty, we also build the courage to *be* honest, and courage is the foundation of all virtues. The courage we equip ourselves with by practicing honest friendship becomes handy elsewhere too.

In this way, honest friendships result in the sharpening of a powerful world-changing weapon. It is not a coincidence that Black feminists like June Jordan and bell hooks were fiercely honest friends *and* fought injustices fiercely.

Polite behavior, June says, is a civility that "grease[s] oppression."[14]

Learning how to wield honesty, you learn how to

puncture a world of deceit, a practice of rinsing until the water runs clear. A willingness to face life truthfully. Untangling yourself from lies, including patriarchal and racist ones that convince us of false inferiorities, changes the world. Actively pursuing honesty within friendships becomes like breathing hot air onto foggy glasses, again, and again, and again, until your surroundings turn crisp and sharp at last.

In the film *The Matrix*, the protagonist Neo is given the choice of a red pill, which would allow him to see his reality truthfully, or a blue pill, which would return him to a state of blissful ignorance. You may prefer the blue pill, because honesty is framed as inherently lonely. We imagine scruff and companionless people who are outcasts. But here is another way to look at it: while you might not make friends in high places—you will not be rewarded by systems of power for probing and questioning them—you will make friends in the right places; good friends will rush around you. Honesty is a gift, not just a burden.

This is not to say honesty is not difficult. You will make mistakes. You might slip into policing friends or being blunt and indelicate. You will struggle striking the right note.

"Her honesty could be harsh," Dr. Malaklou said about bell.

bell was complicated, idiosyncratic, like anyone. She wrote and theorized often about love, but she was often lonely herself. She would get angry at Dr. Malaklou when Dr. Malaklou left to have dinner with her partner and his kids. Why could she not be the locus of Dr. Malaklou's family?

"bell," Dr. Malaklou said, "believed in alternative families, but she recognized that wasn't the world she lived in at the time."

You will get better at it, though. You will learn to reconceptualize what you are being honest about. The "what" is not didactic, it must be dialectic. It is easy to feel entitled to judge, to think you know better, but you may not. Your own viewpoint could be overpowering the picture, disallowing for nuance, or seeing its entirety. What you are being honest about should always be open to challenge, it should always have a question mark—I've noticed this about your situation, what do you think?—not a period. You could be wrong, and in that case, your what should accommodate adjustment. This makes honesty easier. Less scary. You do not have to fling honesty, as though a grenade, and brace for impact, hoping for the best. Honesty can be gentler, more forgiving. Honesty is not hurled, it is offered. Honesty is not delivered as a final draft, but as the first one, open to a friend's edits. Honesty becomes "a repeated game," as my friend Johanne, whose honesty I admire, said. A sort of back-and-forth between friends. Thus, not exploding relationships, but guiding you deeper into them.

Seeing honesty as flexible in this way, strengthens your sense of faith in the friendship. If the what is inflexible, you close your brain off to the reality of time, of a future, in which your what could be adjusted with a friend. If the what is flexible, however, then you must be conscious of time, that you and a friend have more of it, in order to make sense of the what together.

"What enables me to be brave and honest in my friendships is the belief that we have time," Johanne said. "If I hurt them, I trust that they will tell me and that in time, we can reconcile."

You will learn too that honesty is not just about what you are honest about. Honesty is also about how you communicate honesty, and why you are communicating it. What is your intention? Is it in service of your own ego— flexing a sense of authority or superiority over a friend—or is honesty in service of your friend? You can mistakenly focus on the "what," feeling victorious for knowing a truth, without paying attention to how or why that "what" is delivered.

There are a set of choices you face as a friend: does your friend need your honesty, or, more than honesty, does she need your solace and respite? Brutal means "savagely violent," and "honesty" means truthful or correct.[15] We celebrate brutal honesty, but who wants to be savagely violent to a friend? Honesty can feel like a heavy brick. If delivered carelessly, it injures. If delivered thoughtfully, the weight can be shared. You cannot attach the clause "no offense, but…" as insurance, or as immunity from the consequences. Honesty can be delivered compassionately, gently, or not at all, not until a friend is ready. The priority is never honesty alone, but the function of honesty. Will honesty help? Or will it add to a friend's harm? Honesty should always operate to enhance understanding, not more harm.[16]

If you ever feel hesitant about being honest with a friend though, considering the risks, remember dishonesty's aftermath. When a friend spews a harmful belief, saying nothing is like letting her roam with an unlocked weapon, capable of injuring hundreds. Friends must be first in honesty's chain of command.

Actor Tom Holland said in one interview, paraphrasing another actor's advice, "If you have a problem with me, text me. And if you don't have my number, you don't know me well enough to have a problem with me."[17]

If people only accept honesty from people who have their number, then good friendship becomes ever more pressing. When the metaphorical spinach is stuck in a friend's teeth, there is an urgency: it is no one's responsibility to tell her but yours. If you cannot muster the courage to be honest with her, who else will? Who else has the ethos of being in relationship with her to do it?

Holding someone accountable is an act of love, not contempt. To "hold" means to grasp, embrace, or bear another, rather than free-fall.

13.

Friends Far Away

It is hard to cope with distance in friendship. Prominent thinkers have described good friendship as thick and profound, but none clarify the practicalities of its upkeep. If you have good friends, friends who are in it for the right reasons, how do you *stay* in it? How do you keep in touch?

"Keep in touch" is a phrase from the eighteenth century, when soldiers touched shoulders to maintain formation while marching.[1] We cannot always be shoulder to shoulder with friends, life often distances us. You might hit a phase, like parenthood or graduate school that knocks you out of friendship's groove. Physical distance is most common. Jobs and family, which become priorities, never friends, carry you far. Long-distance friendships become inevitable. We are near friends during school, but after, we disperse, like yellow dandelions scattering fuzzy white seeds into the breeze with age.

We are used to friends being nearby, so when they become distant, we think they become unimportant too. Adrienne Torf told me that June would often use the phrase "the decorporealization of relationships," describing how we are becoming increasingly removed from in-person contact; whether having only online friends or ordering things primarily online without human interaction. Decorporealized relationships typically become empty quick. How many social media friends equal one good offline friend? From an average of one hundred and fifty Facebook friends, only four can be relied on in an emotional crisis.[2]

It is wondrous when you feel connected to someone you cannot see, cannot know what they are wearing, or what life-changing event they are experiencing in this very moment. Even while decorporealized, good friends do not hide behind abstractions, niceties, or platitudes, they remain bluntly involved in each other's lives. They still know each other's finances, still know when to cover the bill. Particularities are not a prerequisite for good friendship. Whether a friend stays near or goes far is nonindicative of good friendship. What matters is whether your friendship stays embodied.

Embodied means having, consisting of, or relating to a

physical material body. It is the opposite of decorporealized relationships. Embodied friendships are strong friendships, because although these friends might be far, their friendship feels near.

Nearby friendships are not inherently embodied. Any relationship can become decorporealized—out of touch, empty, superficial, and perfunctory. Nearby friends can lean on physical proximity too much, like a coworker you spend dozens of hours with every week, yet you know little about. Or a roommate you live with but barely speak to. Physical proximity does not ensure good friendship. Nearby friends have a physical certainty, yes, but embodiment is not guaranteed.

Embodied friends, regardless of distance, allow you to feel the friendship's pulse directly inside your body. When long-distance, embodied friends might be oblivious about your life's details, but they stay connected to its contours. These immaterial bonds keep a material firmness between them, like invisible strings, connecting friends no matter their location.

In 44 BCE, Marcus Tullius Cicero wrote the book *Laelius de Amicitia* about friendship (the Latin word for friendship, "amicitia," is where the modern word "amity" comes from). Cicero dedicated *Laelius de Amicitia* to his long-distance childhood friend Atticus. Around one year later, General Marcus Antonius's men intercepted Cicero on his way to a ship heading to Macedonia. Cicero had critiqued Antonius, so Antonius wanted his head. Cicero is said to have extended his neck, telling the soldiers to be swift.[3]

Atticus gruesomely lost his friend, but he preserved Cicero's letters. In these four hundred plus letters, we see an astounding long-distance friendship. We see such a friendship too, over two thousand years later, between Audre Lorde and Pat Parker. Audre was a writer and activist, and Pat was a poet and activist, two of the most influential ones of their time. In one photo of them, they are luminescent, radiating friendship, bodies fitting together like puzzle pieces.[4] Audre and Pat wrote letters to each other too, which are featured in the book *Sister Love: The Letters of Audre Lorde and Pat Parker 1974–1989*, edited by Julie R. Enszer. Together, we can see how, whether in ancient Greece or in contemporary America, whether surviving war, dictatorship, or terminal illness, long-distance friendship can remain embodied, despite there being no bodies close by.

Cicero writes to Atticus, "So far am I from wishing that any one tie between us should be relaxed."[5]

Although not physically together, friendship felt taut between them, a connection stretched and pulled tight—not strained, just firm. In this way, rather than seeing long-distance friendships as second place to nearby ones, as inherently decorporealized friendships that fade with each mile, you can appreciate them as even more miraculous for maintaining embodiment; for preserving a sense of tangible intimacy, despite being intangible.

How do long-distance friendships stay embodied? Through disciplined communication. Consider how hard it was. Pat and Audre were battling cancer. Cicero and Atticus lived during a time of political upheaval. Cicero once wrote, "I write this in haste, being on the march, and with the army."[6] Yet, they still wrote.

People are allergic to the concept of "discipline" in friendships. We treat friendships as light, silly bonds, rather than what they can be: light, silly *and* serious, robust bonds. It is true friendship's beauty is that it is not a romance, it is not greedy, exclusive, or possessive. Yet, that does not mean we should treat friendships so relaxed that they become unimportant.

Disciplined communication first requires clarity about the frequency and style of communication, and this requires discussing expectations. Expectations are premeditated resentments, people say. But this is true only if expectations go uncommunicated. We have such high communication standards with other relationships—you cannot go a day without communicating with your parents, lover, or even your employer without backlash—but there are non-existent standards with friends.

As distant friends, we should set expectations, or a friendship etiquette, just as we do with other important relationships. These expectations can vary: communication styles are different for every friendship. Friendship has its patterns, like increased physically-proximate time at its start to cement familiarity and trust—as Aristotle says, "a wish for friendship may arise quickly, but friendship does not."[7] Afterward, however, there is no standard mold, no quota for how much time to spend, or how to spend that time.

It is similar to common dating advice, you cannot make decisions about marriage or kids by yourself—it depends on *who* you are marrying, *who* you are having kids *with*, that ultimately shapes your opinion. You might never feel like texting one friend but feel like texting another incessantly. You might generally despise phone calls but enjoy phone calls with one friend during your commute home. So long as you are communicating based on a mutually agreed-upon cadence—not FaceTiming a friend annually simply because *she* does not do more—then communication differences are just differences, not value statements.

What matters most is committing to whatever rhythm

suits your friendship best, whether talking every day, biweekly, monthly, or whenever you read a good book and forward her an excerpt to discuss. Whatever your communication style might be—and it should always be open to revision—consistent communication is what keeps friendships embodied, no matter how far or near.

You will mess up, of course. Audre writes to Pat, "When I did not receive an answer to my letter last spring, I took a long and painful look at the 15 years we have known each other and decided that I had to accept the fact that we would never have the openness of friendship I always thought could be possible being the two strong Black women we are, with all our differences and samenesses. Then your card from Nairobi, and I thought once again maybe when I'm out there next spring Pat and I will sit down once and for all and look at why we were not more available to each other all these years. I was overjoyed to get your letter and what it means in your life. There are conversations we need to have, Pat, each for her own clarity, and neither one of us has forever."

Pat writes, "I feel somewhat hampered trying to communicate by writing a letter. I look forward to the time when you and I can sit down for a very long period of time and talk out a lot of the things that have been happening to us and happening between us."[8]

Cicero writes to Atticus, "I get letters from you far too seldom considering that you can much more easily find people starting for Rome than I to Athens: considering, too, that you are more certain of my being at Rome than I of your being at Athens."[9]

But messing up is not a catastrophe. When a good friend does not meet your expectations, repercussions are never punitive, because the fundamental belief that she loves you is never undermined. You trust each other, trust that your disappointment is not because of malicious intent but rather miscommunication, and so you talk.

The second key element is not just any diligent communication, but *vulnerable* communication. Over time, as the dates on June Jordan's archived papers moved from the sixties to the nineties, then the two thousands, letters turned into faxes, which turned into emails. Today, our communication is mostly calls and texts. The ease of communication today is nice but also dangerous. You can get away with doing little. You can send a lot of noise with a flick of a finger without saying much. Modern communication mediums lend themselves to *invulnerable* communication. While social media is useful in maintaining friendships, strictly social media friendships are empty. And they are designed to be. Deep and challenging friendships do not make social media companies money, entertaining ones do.

If you are not vulnerable, you add emotional distance onto the physical distance. When good friendships become distant you might share highlight reels, or brush discontent under the rug, either because of lazy friendship-ing, or, a logic that hard conversations will strain a bond already strained by distance. But if you treat friendships like glass, they become like glass. Friendships become fragile, unwelcoming to human complexity. In a friendship where you have already established trust, vulnerability does not detract from friendships, it deepens them.

We should be vigilant about not just whether we are communicating consistently with friends, but *how* we are communicating. Pat and Audre and Cicero and Atticus did not write any letters, they attempted being fully themselves in those letters. Not censoring themselves for easy consumption. Mutual vulnerability in addition to consistent communication is what seals good friendships, even if far away.

When you find your rhythm, long-distance friendship can soar into an unrivaled intimacy. Keeping in touch stops being a chore. No longer reactionary to your immediate life—in other words, only a space for catching up—the immaterial friendship space that you build becomes its own thing. A spiritual rather than physical space pulsing deep inside the recesses of your brains. It gains its own sensation, its own smell and imagery, like a room suspended in another plane, which only you both have the code to. You know long-distance friends have discovered this sweet spot when they become effusive, eager to enter their metaphysical friendship space. Eager to linger.

Cicero writes to Atticus, "I have absolutely nothing to say to you. You know everything, nor can I expect any fresh news from you. Let me, then, merely maintain my old habit of never letting anyone going to you depart without a letter."[10]

In another letter, "I have been talking politics with you all this time, and I would have gone on doing so, had not my lamp failed me."[11]

And in another, "Yes, pray write to me frequently just anything that comes into your head."[12]

Pat writes to Audre, "I have no idea where to begin this letter. There are so many thoughts, and fears, and emotions moving within me that I feel like a nuclear reactor out of control."[13]

Audre writes, astounded by how much she was sharing, "Now. I wish I could have this letter self-destruct like *Mission: Impossible*, but I can't, so don't please leave it lying around."

Pat had to stop herself once, as many of us feel when conversing in the metaphysical space with a good friend. "Enough. This is turning into a book."[14]

The room has so much flavor, liveliness, and influence that, despite spending more time apart than together, you feel your friend's closeness. Her person earns a tangible quality to it, causing you to think, what would she say, what would she think, what would she do if she was here now?

Even absent, a long-distance friend's presence can change your life's trajectory. Cicero once wrote to Atticus on board a ship. He was contemplating fleeing Rome, because he knew his life was in danger. Yet, he did not flee: Atticus's words in a previous letter—"Can you with honour, you who talk of a noble death—can you with honour abandon your country?"—were ringing in his ears. He turned back around.[15]

The funny thing about good communication is that, when done with consistency and vulnerability, it allows friends to not communicate at all too, when need be. In these particular scenarios, a forewarned absence of communication does not signal dying friendship, but a hearty one. The trust between you is so strong that friendship survives even if unattended to.

Poet, cultural worker, and educator Kathy Engel, June Jordan's friend, told me, "My closest friends, we have an understanding. If it's going to be awhile until one of us hears from another, we'll let each other know what's going on. We trust. I sometimes say, I can't call you back, my voice is really tired. I know friends who put friends on hold for several months, because they're working on something important. This trust doesn't come overnight in a friendship, but with those close friends you slowly develop enough of understanding that you give each other some grace."

Long-distance friendships are not guaranteed to become decorporealized barren bonds fading day by day, mile by mile. Embodied friendship is when friends still feel each other in their hearts and minds, whether close or not. They do not go slack. Although the shell of friendship evolves with changing cities, jobs, and countries, the essence stays the same. You do not have to settle in faraway friendships. These friendships can be stronger than even nearby ones, because they operate on a remarkable trust and showcase a relentless effort, a precious desire for friendship regardless of one's circumstances.

It should be noted, long-distance friendship still requires some in-person time. Audre and Pat called, stayed in each other's homes, *and* wrote letters. Cicero and Atticus visited each other, too. In-person time births memories, which constitutes much of friendship's magnetic pull. Remember that time in college when we...? That time on Judah Street and we saw...? If your reminiscing stays rooted too far in the past, never catching up to the present, your bond is never the main site of action, only the reconnaissance. Friendship suffers without the memorial glue—the inside jokes, the "remember whens"—needed to adjoin two physically separated people together.

In-person time helps resurrect friendship, if you feel its pulse slowing. Looking into the distance, you might hear howling wind, only to see emptiness. When you meet a long-distance friend, you remind each other of each other, you nurse each other back into friendship.

Cicero told Atticus straightforwardly when he needed to see his friend in the flesh. He once wrote, "If I once had your ears to listen to me, I could unburden myself in the conversation of a single walk...."[16]

You do not have to keep in touch with every friend. Some friendships have natural endings and changing seasons. But, if distance settles between you and a friend, you do not *have* to surrender friendship. You can ruthlessly convey an intention to be friends with disciplined and vulnerable communication. With these ingredients, even distant friends will remain close.

We think long-distance friendships are worse, because with physical distance must come emotional distance too. But you can learn to appreciate long-distance friendship as another genre of good friendship. We can let friends go, without letting go of their hands.

In 1989, at the age of forty-five, Pat died from breast

cancer. Three years later, at the age of fifty-eight, Audre died, also from breast cancer.

Less than one year before her death, Pat wrote, "Audre love, This is not a piece of paper, but my arm extending across all the damn miles between us to hold you and hug you with all the strength, we have had to gain from the pain. This is my hand reaching inside you to feel the hole that is there. Right now I feel betrayed by words; there is nothing I can say that says what I feel."

When friends are nearby, we think we have them. Good, embodied friendship is not exclusive to physical closeness, however, but a product of deep vulnerability and discipline. When friends are far away, we think we lose them. But long-distance friendships can be extraordinarily embodied, too. They are not destined for decorporealization. Vulnerability and discipline blasts through any distance.

After Pat died, Audre stayed in touch, despite never being able to touch Pat again. Audre wrote to Pat's partner, Martha Dunham, "I loved her so much, Marty, and I feel her with me smiling so often…when I promised her I would be whatever you needed me to be after she was gone (in our last telephone conversation) I meant it. Whatever."[17]

Their friendship lasted even after death fashioned permanent distance.

14.

Goodbye, Friend

FRIENDSHIP BREAKUPS ARE not commonly discussed, but they are devastating. They are even more taboo than romantic breakups. While romantic breakups bring you closer to others, uniting with friends and family around breakup songs and rituals, friendship breakups do not.[1] Whereas romantic breakups are forced into meaning, because they culminate into you finding "the one," friendship breakups have no larger purpose, do not signal anything but inadequacy or failure. You keep it hush. You worry about social contagion: other friends realizing your undesirability, too. When someone closest to you rejects you, your heart drops. Pain blossoms through your chest. It wounds deeply.

Scrolling through my phone, I see photos of a childhood

friend scrunching her nose, tongue out, taking selfies while sipping lemonade. I see her napping, head in my mom's lap. There she is on my driveway, colorful chalk spread out, looking over her shoulder, making a peace sign. A video of her stranded in art class. A photo of her adjusting her hair. A shaky video of us, elated, reconvening from summer vacation.

I remember what we did not capture too, arguments so resounding, so stabbing, that I left her parents' house once and returned to mine. There, absentmindedly, I stirred an extra cup of lemonade, only to realize, turning around, that there was nobody to hand it to.

"Certain friendships can feel like threads in the fabric of our lives, anchor points to our memories, and can become synonymous with our identities at certain junctures," says clinical psychologist Dr. Arianna Brandolini. "When we lose them, it can feel like we lose a part of ourselves."[2]

Society disenfranchises us of our pain, but not only is losing a friend painful, how we lose them is, too. We have nonchalant terms like "friendscaping," or the pruning of friendships that are dead weight in our metaphorical social garden. Although friendscaping signals intentional and non-passive relationship-ing, it is still insensitive. Friends are not branches to be clipped with garden scissors. If a romantic partner breaks up with you via text, it is widely admonished. When a friend breaks up with you though, not even a text is required. We believe we owe friends nothing. Ghosting is regular. On top of the social shame, friendship breakups can be torturously ambiguous, offering little closure.

One of Spain's most celebrated contemporary novelists, Javier Marías, wrote a piece in 2018, when he was sixty-seven years old, titled, "When and Why Did We Stop Seeing Each Other? I Simply Don't Know."

Sure, he had friendships that ended jarringly, because of a mutual disliking and disillusionment. Yet, "far more difficult to understand are the cases where, if I can put it like this, nothing happened: there were no betrayals, no disenchantments or quarrels, not even a sense of weariness."

Javier had a friend, Michi Panero. After Michi died, Javier realized that despite spending every day together once, somehow, their friendship lost its freshness and withered. There was also Gustavo Pérez de Ayala, who Javier visited daily in Gustavo's mother's apartment in calle de Padilla, a street in Madrid, Spain. Staring at Gustavo's obituary, Javier again wondered, when had they become strangers?

"When and why did we stop seeing each other, Michi and I, Gustavo and I? I simply don't know."[3]

Part of why friendship breakups lack conceptualization

and cultural significance is then because they often go unnoticed. They are rarely documented; most are undramatic and nebulous. Often, there is no "breakup," no punctual moment of ruin. Nothing exactly disastrous happens, friends unwind gradually. Many romantic relationships are premised on exclusivity and monogamy. When a relationship ends, one lover is replaced with another, so you can better trace and demarcate the relationship's ending. Since friendships are non-exclusive, the rift, and maybe the tragedy, is harder to perceive.

This can make you feel anxious and unresolved, but what if, instead, we learned to appreciate friendship's ambiguousness? Its open-endedness.

Friendship breakups help us deal with a deep insecurity as humans: accepting that love is not possession. Accepting this, means relinquishing entitlement, assuming a humility about what is in your control, and what is not. You can never secure an airtight, lifelong grip on a friend (you can never secure an airtight grip on anyone, including a spouse, although marriage tricks us into believing otherwise). Non-possessive love can feel scary, anxiety-inducing, because it is uncontrollable. But we all are in a relationship with time, nobody is exempt. Love is not possession, but it is many other things, including the courage to love even amid the uncertainty time weaves around you and your beloved.

Friendship is deeply nonlinear. Not only are the methods of breakups murky, the difference between a breakup and a disagreement can be too, adding to the uncertainty. For instance, June and Adrienne Rich broke up for around three years before finding their way back to friendship. June and Frances Fox Piven broke up for a while, too.

In a 2011 interview, Frances said, "June and I were really very close. There were times when we were not so close, although we remained lifelong friends."[*]

In most romantic relationships, you have two options: break up forever, or get married. With friends, it is not binary. This can be maddeningly vague, but again, it can also be exemplary. You are forced to unlearn possessiveness, and thus, unlearn linear narratives. If something is nonlinear, capitalism says it is unproductive. We learn to move from Point A to Point B as efficiently as possible, because our capitalist society wants streamlined workers, not "lazy" ones. Yet, I think of my friend who walks to work taking the *least* efficient route. She says she enjoys it more, freeing herself from society's obsessions about destinations and end products, both of which are about profit—as opposed to journeys, which are about people, in other words, about *us*. Nonlinearity is unproductively precious. Full of surprises. You cannot predict your path. Friendship requires "continued, mutual forgiveness," as

Irish Poet David Whyte says; we are woefully unequipped
to be friends, and there is heavy systemic pushback against
friendship, which increases our likelihood of messing up.[5]
Your breakup might be for a few years, decades, or forever.
With friendship, you cannot know, and that is the wonder
of it.

Sometime after June ended her friendship with Frances
Fox Piven during a painful lunch in New York City, June's
son called her. He recommended Frances's new book, *Poor
People's Movements: Why They Succeed, How They Fail.*

June had not spoken to Frances since their breakup,
but she bought the book anyway, finishing it in almost one
sitting.

"And I decided to let it stand," she writes. "To let the
failures of friendship stand and to reach out, instead, to
Frances in areas of mutual, urgent concern, to engage once
again in talk about tactics of struggle."

Before picking up the phone to dial Frances, June hes-
itated. Then, she thought, "What the hell; friendship is not
a tragedy; we can be polite." And so she called Frances up,
"to talk."[6]

A benefit of there being no cultural scripts for friendship breakups, is that the idea of a total break that often
characterizes romantic breakups does not haunt them.
There is a chance of reconciliation. A friendship breakup

is not a definite tragedy. If it feels right, you can dial a friend again. The possibility for friends to reenter your life, because friendships are non-exclusive, unlike many romantic relationships, does not mean closing a friendship door is impossible. Rather, if mutually agreed upon, then there is a plasticity, an opportunity unique to friendship to try again. We should remember though, when something breaks, even when glued back together, a crack often remains. The friendship will never be the same. So although friendship breakups have no determined timeline, we should not treat them casually.

Even if we never open that door again, we can still celebrate a finished friendship. I try not to feel bewildered when a friendship ends. Friendship breakups are not failures. So-called failed friendships are as equally meaningful as long-lasting ones—what we think of as "successful" friendships.

The Combahee River Collective disbanded in 1980. Friendships drifted; people went their separate ways.

One of its founders, Demita Frazier, said, "The Combahee lived its life and had a natural beginning and end. That's why I said there was no big blow up, no big fight, no internal schism. People's politics just diverged. But I'd never been a part of anything that had such a profound impact on my life."[7]

The time you spent, even if not a lifetime, is not wasted time. A good friendship is not always a forever friendship. Best friends are not always best friends forever. In a capitalist culture that loves ownership and definiteness for things that are inherently unownable and indefinite, this is again a profound stance. We want people and things to last, to possess them, in order for them to mean something. But things die. It is natural. When a relationship ends, it does not end in meaning. We have notions that everything is for life, adorning bracelets with terms like BFF, or best friend forever, but why are those the rules of friendship? As my friend Nastasia points out, would you not adopt a pet, just because you will outlive them? There is value in relationships that do not last forever, too.

Sometimes, no matter how good of a friend you are, friendships nevertheless end permanently. We understand that romantic relationships can end because of incompatibilities unindicative of people's characters, but when friendships end explicitly, people talk. Since there are so few obligations to friends, when a friendship terminates, as opposed to simply fading, people presume a giant rupture. But a friendship ending explicitly is not always a sign of catastrophe. Friendships do not always end due to negative changes, but because of neutral changes too. You do not have to villainize a friend to make your breakup intelligible.

A friendship breakup can be a sign of intentionality, not just explosion. Intentionally closing a friendship as opposed to continuing it insincerely. This brightens the prospect of breakups. Rather than clinging onto passive friendships, you acknowledge their natural conclusions; that stagnant bonds can prevent friends from growing, even if that means growing apart.

Two good people are not always good together. Maybe ideas that once enveloped you in conversations for hours, no longer do, due to shifting interests. Maybe your attitudes and aspirations in life have changed, and you disagree more, not in ways where one person is right, and the other is wrong, but in ways where you butt heads too regularly, creating an exhausting dynamic. Love is loyalty to another's well-being, which means the loving friend is willing to step away from the friendship when your well-beings are no longer nurtured by each other.

Sometimes though, there *are* negative changes in friends. We grow up with a famous example: Judas was Jesus's friend. One day, in the garden of Gethsemane, he approaches Jesus as he prays, placing a kiss on Jesus's cheek, identifying him to the authorities, and condemning him to crucifixion. Regret quickly swarms Judas like hornets. He returns his reward of thirty pieces of silver to the authorities, and he hangs himself.

For the rest of us, unamiable friendship breakups are perhaps more subtle. Ruthlessness makes friends see red, jealousy turns them green. I once learned that a friend of mine was secretly rooting for me to fail. I remained in the friendship, however, because I had known her since kindergarten.

An economics concept is the sunk-cost fallacy, when past investments into something prevent you from leaving it. Say you drive hours to buy a coat, but you find on the tag that it is not your size. Considering the long drive, leaning into the sunk-cost fallacy—a common psychological hindrance to letting go—you purchase it anyway. At home, you squeeze into it, unable to breathe because it is so tight, until you realize you must drive over again to buy another one.[8]

I had to realize that no matter a friendship's uniqueness or lengthiness, when a friendship has run its course, you save yourself trouble by concluding it. Let go or be dragged, as they say.

You might worry that the window for making new friends has passed, which encourages you to cling. But friendship is not a Hollywood romance, where (supposedly) the good ones get gradually taken. Old friends may age like wine, but new friends can glisten without the baggage of time. As you end friendships, you make space for new ones, too. Optimism shines faintly in the possibility of new friendships, whenever you are ready. We think of good friends as scarce resources, people we meet in childhood and stick to. But friendship, if we are open to it, can be formed just as deep and blazing at any age.

Friendship does require continued forgiveness, but there comes a point when always forgiving "becomes not an act of moral strength," writes essayist Maria Popova, "but one of moral weakness—an exercise in self-mutilation in the unwillingness to relinquish what has metastasized into a draining or even abusive relationship."[9]

Writer John Steinbeck was close friends with George Albee. Until he realized George was only feigning friendship. In reality, George was deeply jealous of John's career, fanning rumors behind John's back. John wrote George a letter to cement their breakup—a rare public example of a friendship breakup.

John tells George that he has had enough. He is sick of George twisting his words "viciously," spreading them until they ultimately circle back to him, like a bad game of telephone.

"I tried to sidestep, just to fade out of your picture," John writes. "But that doesn't work either. I'd like to be friends with you, George, but I can't if I have to wear a mail shirt the whole time."[10]

Just because friendship is a vague social category,

does not mean you are obligated to call everyone a friend. Friendship, unlike romantic relationships, which legalize control and possession ("until death do us part"), disciplines us in the delicate art of holding on *and* letting go. Friendship forces a keen awareness of your feelings, which is useful in a society that desensitizes us, causing tolerance of mediocrity, numbing us into passivity toward injustice too. Friendship teaches that when you enter relationships, you can exit them as well. You cannot get married to friends, and that is the beauty of it. You never sit passively in friendships, you never take them for granted, which is a lesson for every relationship. Once a friend, does not mean always a friend. Although friendships are among our deepest relationships, you do not have to abandon what is important to you, like goodness and kindness, for the sake of company, especially when friends change for the worse.

When I was twelve years old, I tidied chalk pastels into a box, rubbed my colorful fingertips against my T-shirt, and left without turning around, without realizing that I would never return to this place where I learned how to draw an oval, and eventually a face. When one of my good friends was four years old, she released her babysitter's hand inside an empty kitchen in Singapore and waddled away, without turning around, without realizing her family was moving to the US the next day.

Forks in the road are natural, I remember thinking,

hugging this childhood friend, knowing our friendship has ended. Our infant fantasies, that we can draw all day, that we can always hold her hand, are quickly ruptured. When we think of goodbyes, we think of train stations, World War II, a girl running with a flapping handkerchief after a boy, a soldier, becoming smaller and smaller on a departing train. How do friends say goodbye, though?

Even if a friendship ends under more negative circumstances, we can say goodbye by resisting seeing it as a failure of friendship as a whole. After my childhood friendship ended, whenever I remembered her, I felt sour. But for a relationship to be meaningful, it does not have to last. Aristotle writes that when friends break up, the memory of your friend still keeps you company.[11] You never really lose a friend in this way. Your past friendship—the laughs you shared, the trust you once felt—remain etched in time, untainted by whatever is happening now. You can still love the friend you once had, the friendship that you once shared, while letting go of who a friend has become now. You might be itchy to remove, disentangle, and erase her. But you cannot. Good friendship changes your body chemistry. This is evidence of a good friendship's success, even if unsuccessful in time. Do not turn misanthropic or pessimistic; instead, we must pick ourselves up and carry on, parting ways with a friend, but not with friendship itself.

15.

Boundaries

IN THE TUDOR era, friends shared gravestones. Many philosophers believed in this kind of interchangeability between friends, as scholar Ivy Schweitzer explains: Aristotle believed a friend is a "double," or "second self;" Cicero, in 44 BCE, thought of friends as "one soul or mind in two bodies;" Michel de Montaigne, a philosopher during the French Renaissance, believed that "friends are not merely bonded, but 'fused' and 'confused,'" and their "souls mingle and blend with each other so completely that they efface the seam that joined them, and cannot find it again."[1]

My cousin drove me to San Francisco from the South Bay. She was thirty-three, single, and content. One hand on the wheel, the other moving expressively, she shared that her friends were stuck in "unhappy marriages."

When she said "unhappy marriages," I thought about my friendship with Winona. After graduation, we had moved in together, secure in our vision to pursue social change as we had since high school.

My cousin stopped outside our apartment in Haight-Ashbury.

Blowing a kiss, she drove off.

Instead of walking inside, I walked away, toward Buena Vista Park, which protruded like a green camel's hump from the city, the Pacific rumbling behind it. It was a steep hike. Up top, the Golden Gate Bridge shimmered a red I had never seen before, rich and romantic.

I wondered why I thought of Winona when my cousin said unhappy marriages.

I was never hesitant to spend 24-7 with Winona, to live with her, move across the country with her, introducing her to my family, friends, and professors. And she did the same. We aspired for no boundaries, believing it was okay, since we are friends, not those romantic couples who disappear into each other, collapsing into themselves. The limits of their world shrinking.

We would make coffee together, work on our nonprofit—signing our emails "W&P"—work out together, make lunch, work some more in the living room, cook dinner for each other, then repeat. I noticed the equation of romantic relationships—shared daily rituals, entirely cocreated networks resulting in few relationships of one's own, and partners crawling into every crevice of every thought—and I replaced friends into that equation instead.

My friend Nastasia, who had once lived with a childhood friend, described feeling unreasonably upset when this friend broke their apartment shower. If it was anyone else, she would have laughed. But with this friend, she recalled previous upsets, and her memories compounded into a feeling: something knotted and tangled. For Winona and me, little things triggered unresolved conflicts from our extensive time together. I started feeling unempathetic toward her. We tried frequent communication, but the continuous heavy discussions felt overwhelming, like swimming in molasses, ceaselessly excavating our childhood traumas and wielding them as explanations for our irrational, ugly behavior. One day, after Winona's friend Maya visited for the weekend, I asked Winona how she felt seeing her.

"We laughed a lot."

Closing my bedroom door, something heavy sat on my chest. A recognition of loss. I missed laughing with Winona.

Studies show that social cohesion, a commitment to others, is good for your health. Too much cohesion, however, devolves into enmeshment. Therapist Salvador

Minuchin coined "enmeshment" to describe "overinvolved" relationships without boundaries; most common in families, either parental-child or marital relationships.[2]

This can happen in friendships, too. Enmeshment creates a similar sticky excessive reliance. While I was proud of how Winona and I repeatedly chose each other, I started wondering, had we gone too far? In seeking to uplift friendship, did we wrongfully disregard our selfhood? Would Winona leave? Or would I—could I? And if we did drift apart, what would I do then, having centered my life so sincerely around Winona?

I thought friendships were safe under some shield, unhealthy dynamics skirting overhead but never reaching inside. But you can spend too much time with friends, too. You can overextend yourself for a friend, too. Merely substituting friends into the status quo does not "change or subvert" the status quo.[3] In seeking to uplift friendship, you can wrongfully disregard yourself, doing exactly what couples experiencing a violent consumption by their partners do: become enmeshed. And discontent.

You know whether a friendship is enmeshed through compassion. In enmeshed friendships, friends turn slightly monstrous. Unable to understand each other, impatient, and excessively critical or unforgiving. Compassion is missing because you cannot conceptualize each other as separate people. You stand *so* close, you no longer see.

It would take a lot to stir an emotional response in me when something happened in Winona's life. When you melt into another person, they become a casualty of the disregard we may have for ourselves. Our enmeshment made me wonder, what is it that a friend can do, that you cannot do yourself, that is then lost when a friend becomes part of yourself?

Enmeshment is dangerous, but you should not rush toward the opposite either: individualism. If enmeshment is when two people become one, individualism is when two people on one planet pretend they live on separate ones. Enmeshed relationships suck you too deep into others, but individualistic ones pull you too far away.

Individualism is lonely, the exchange of community for ego. My dad has a fridge magnet with an Aristotle quote: "Knowing yourself is the beginning to all wisdom." He taps it often. Remember. Instead of overanalyzing the interpersonal when disappointed, focus on self-centering. Pay attention to how you react, and why. It is all you can do.

But knowing yourself cannot happen *by yourself.* Self-centering cannot mean self-isolation. Selfhood cannot be broken off from your surroundings. The self, or the individual, is always a social thing. It is a multiplicitous and ever-changing process, where one's self ultimately comes into view through the polishing presence of others.

To avoid enmeshed friendships, we can aim for autonomous friendships instead. Autonomy and individualism are different. Individualism is about an external worldview, imagining yourself as unrelated to society. Autonomy, a branch of individualism, is an internal worldview.[*] It is about embracing the need for self-expression and self-determination, even while seeing yourself as *part* of society.

Imagine two friends walking down the street, tired. A bed magically appears, but only one person can sleep in it. If the friends are individualists, they would break into a run, shouting, "first come, first serve!" Whoever reaches the bed first, sleeps, the other stays awake. If the friends are enmeshed, if both could not sleep, none of them would, because they operate as one entity. If they are autonomous, however, they would articulate their individuality. One friend might say she ran ten miles. Could she sleep first? Recognizing her greater need, the other friend would step aside, inviting her to rest.

In this way, you can prioritize autonomy—a recognition of individual and diverse needs and desires between friends—while still prioritizing relationships. Embracing autonomy means a more conscious kind of friendship-ing, a sensitivity to friends' individuality, even while you embrace your togetherness. Individualism, on the other hand, means always choosing yourself (the individual) over your friend, regardless of her needs and desires.

Autonomy is critical. Autonomy, or the lack of, is political. Injustice normalizes the elimination of certain people's autonomy. Instead, politically vulnerable people are overdetermined by their context: twenty-four US states, as of 2024, stripped autonomy from trans, nonbinary, and gender-diverse people, restricting gender-affirming care like psychological support and medical interventions; in other words, your autonomy is ignored, you have no say over your choices about your own body.[5] Married women once had no legal identities or rights to their wages, children, or bodies; marital rape was not criminalized until the 1980s, and the Supreme Court just overturned *Roe v. Wade*, denying people rights to abortion, or, again, denying people autonomy over their own bodies.[6]

Women in my family take care of everyone, running from one family member to another, despite doctor warnings that their blood pressures are prematurely high from stress. When learning what it means to be a woman, you learn it means to be overly giving, always caretaking, never autonomous. But I do not want to, as philosopher Trudy Govier says, "disappear into derivative relational identities such as daughter, wife, and mother," and, although I once believed it was valiant, not into the derivative identity of friend, either.[7]

Friendship is susceptible to the threat of disappearing women, too.

Autonomy is not a bad word. Practicing autonomy in your friendship strengthens a political ethic. Just like a healthy friendship, a healthy solidarity, at a larger scale, does not mean blotting out individuality, refusing people's singularity under the name of one suffocating, blurring "unity." Solidarity means coming together while also being vigilant about what sets you apart, what makes people different, what makes some more vulnerable than others. Autonomy, in balance, prioritizes coming together without total erasure.

When June said, after visiting the Sabra and Shatila Palestinian refugee camps, "I was born a Black woman / and now / I am become a Palestinian...," she was not conveying an enmeshment with her Palestinian friends, a total fusion of identities, but rather an intimacy that appreciates differences and distances.[8] Only if she could *see* these differences could she see Palestinians' specific struggle.

Insisting on self-determination, on some autonomy, is not selfish. It does not interfere with a larger vision of friendship, it informs it. It is not one or another, selflessness or self-interestedness, there is an interplay, a reciprocity between the two. You can balance them, a dependence on friends and a wish for some independence. You can exercise autonomy without relinquishing love and friendship.

At the point of juncture, where you connect with a friend, remembering autonomy means not forgoing yourself, liquefying into one amorphous being; instead asking, *How can I love you, how can you love me, and how should I be loving myself?*

Enmeshment is an unhealthy recipe for intimacy, with a lineage in denying people autonomy at the expense of their domination and exploitation. Never allowed the boldness of your own needs. You can break this cycle in your friendships. The kind of loving friends should strive for is one where love does not equal sameness, but an in-tune-ness of heart that leaps forward and connects us despite where you are, or what you are doing, whether you are together or apart.

Autonomy does not mean excoriating a friend. It means seriously centering friends in the wake of friendship's systematic devaluation, but, before placing an oxygen mask on her, securing yours first. It means setting boundaries, especially when a lack of boundaries is gendered. Boundaries include saying no, allowing independent identities, interests, and relationships, and giving voice to your personal limits.

Researcher and author Brené Brown describes how, *without* boundaries, you become resentful and hateful, assuming, "people [are] sucking on purpose just to piss me off." With boundaries, however, by being straightforward about "what's okay and what's not okay," space opens up for generosity. For assuming that people are doing their best. Boundaries prevent burnout. With boundaries, you become better equipped to "tread that water" of compassion forever.[9]

By setting boundaries, you reclaim autonomy in a society that drowns people with marginalized identities in obligatory enmeshment. Boundaries do not draw you inward, away from community, but facilitate a more sustainable loving toward it.

I watched a television taping of acclaimed writers James Baldwin and Maya Angelou. James wears a mustard yellow dress shirt, a brown and beige print scarf knotted fashionably around his neck. He sits at a table with Maya, who wears a brown jacket over an apricot pink blouse, with plates, food, and drink between them. Maya juts her chin out and grins. James smiles ear to ear, flashing the endearing gap between his front teeth. Both puff their cigarettes while talking, swirling their hands emphatically.

Maya asks James why he lives in the South of France, why he made that decision when he loves his family in the United States so much.

James says, "[France is] not exactly my home. It's a kind of asylum. It's a place where I can work. I have a lot of work to do. And if you are in the situation where you're always resisting and resenting, it's very hard to—"

Maya said, "It takes too much energy."

"Well you can't write a book," James said.

"No."

"You can't write a sentence."

James had important work to do, and he had to be alive to do it. He barely knew anyone his own age. His friends, like Dr. Martin Luther King Jr. and Malcolm X, had been killed.

I think back to how June Jordan escaped to a Long Island cabin in the wilderness, seeking to replicate great American men's lifestyles. I remember how, after being assaulted, feeling lonely and sick of the isolation, June vowed to return to the city. Her move to Long Island differed from James's move to France because June sought individualism, quickly realizing how unconscionable and impractical it was, while James sought autonomy. The difference was, in asserting autonomy as opposed to individualism, James never dismissed his interconnectedness.

"We have paid for this country," James says to Maya. "That's why I can never leave it, by the way…I've never deluded myself into thinking that."[10]

He chose a solitude that was *in service of* solidarity. We think solitude and solidarity are opposites, just as we think autonomy and friendship are, but they are not. June, like most of us, made the mistake of choosing one, thinking it comes at the cost of the other. But they do not.

James could have felt like a failure, because he was unable to match the supposedly supreme model of intimacy—enmeshment, or losing himself (literally, even if it led to death) in his relationships, like with his family or with his friends, such as Maya, who he now had to write to all the way from France. But good friendship requires autonomy, not enmeshment. This is why I think James's friends and family let him go.

Winona and I needed room to change, to experience and experiment, which our fierce commitment did not make space for. When my cousin said unhappy marriages, I thought of Winona because we *were* operating like a marriage, breaking down our identities into a singular entity, and that *did* make us unhappy. We felt like failures, because we felt unable to be enmeshed, as meaningful relationships are advertised to be. Turns out, we were not failing, but the model was failing us. We were jamming friendship into a mold that arrived broken. Loving means respecting someone enough to insist on autonomy, a relational kind of autonomy, rather than a total desertion of self. Our intention was to love each other in a society that neglects friends, and so Winona and I prioritized each other—even if at the expense of our individual well-being.

"And if I held you back, at least I held you close," sings The Weeknd.

In a status quo that disregards friends, as adults, not many have actively pursued friendship to the extent of enmeshment. I do not wish to denounce the importance of togetherness, only to flag an important way to consider oneself amid its passions: autonomy, or taking care of yourself.

Winona walked into our apartment. I just made myself lunch. I opened my bedroom door, fork in hand, and leaned against the doorframe. Cheeks red from San Francisco's winds, she unlaced her Doc Martens, sharing this week's stories: a night shift at a gay bar, last Saturday's park meditation, and her progress on the library books crowding her bedroom. We were laughing again, I realized. My enmeshment with her had meant I was fixed on who I thought she was, without being present to who she is becoming.

Friends should not wrangle difference into sameness. Good friends glisten in their individuality (note, not individualism). You should hold friends accountable, but not to the extent of sacrificing autonomy for accountability. You should truth-tell always, but also keep your opinions tame about friends' ultimate choices—so long as they are not causing harm—rather than feeling shocked, personally slighted, or abandoned after.[11] You should want friends to feel ample room to change, able to wander through life's paths in pursuit of love and justice, unrushed. You want friends to feel supported, not suffocated, which enmeshment, even if coming from a place of fierce commitment, will not make space for.

To be a good friend, you must also be a friend to yourself. In friendships moments of deepest intimacy, you should see friendship as an asymptotic process, drawing near, but never converging. Advancing an attitude that disrupts binaries: loving yourself cannot happen alone, *and* loving yourself requires having a "self" to begin with. Rather than effacing the seam that unites you, as French philosopher Michel de Montaigne says about friendship, honoring that a seam brings two things together, but also holds them apart, ever so slightly.

16.

Just Friends

WHICH IS YOUR favorite, the last book you read or this one? Which is your favorite, the last city you visited or this one? These were my favorite questions as a child. Something was always better, something always worse. It is maybe why, when I began writing this book in college, good friends reigned supreme. They were my favorite. It was good friends or no friends.

A person's social network can be surprisingly complex; many of us, though, stick to hierarchical thinking. Like a pyramid, we imagine those closest to us at the apex, everybody else taking second, third, or fourth place beneath them.

Rather than ranking friendships into a vertical hierarchy, each kind a block climbing into a pyramid's apex (good friends), what if we unstacked them? Rather than vertical thinking, what if we thought horizontally? Friendships are more like a jigsaw puzzle, not a pyramid. One piece is not greater than another. Some differ in sizes, some form the borders, some snap into place within the center, but every irregular piece together forms a complete picture.

I met someone at a party. She jumped onto my bus, accompanying me on the ride back to my apartment. Friendship requires effort, but also luck. Luck, such as chemistry. An attraction to a friend; qualities you admire, even if it is, at minimum, her desire to be a good friend. I felt a spark with this person. My bus stop was approaching, and I felt it was approaching too fast. We shouted over the noise, heads leaning in. City lights splashed colors onto our faces. My eyes darted nervously to the stop names flashing in pixelated yellow letters by the driver's head. Exchanging numbers in a rush, she then sputtered something, which brings me to the second element of friendship's required luck: the tremendous luck that you both can be good friends to each other.

She was moving across the world.

Long-distance, as we have discussed, does not necessarily curtail the possibilities of good friendship. But I was tired, bogged down by an injury that left little space for growing a new good friendship, especially one in an opposite time zone.

I once would have let her go. For me, it was good friends or nothing—what was the point of a half-hearted friendship? But I am learning otherwise. You will meet people who are good friends, but cannot be a good friend *to you*, whether because of their job, geography, health, or their commitments to the good friends that they already have. I am not arguing for lazy friendships here, but rather, for nuance. Mismatched life paths cause missed opportunities. Instead of becoming good friends, these people can become just friends. Or maybe something between "stranger," "acquaintance," and "friend," but we do not have the words yet.

"The limits of my language," philosopher Ludwig Wittgenstein writes, "mean the limits of my world."[1]

They are still good bonds, trusting and consistent, neither person using the other for pleasure or utility, neither superficially interested in the other, but neither are they as tightly wound as your good friendships are. You share a meal with them now and then; you call them once in a while. These bonds are meaningful too—imperative even, within an ecosystem of relationships. And in this ecosystem, nobody is greater than, nobody is less than. It is not a competition, but, together, a constellation that the people in our lives illuminate. It is not a pyramid, but a puzzle. What this does is train our brains to unlearn hierarchy. Just because a good bond in your life is not a good friendship, you should not discredit it. Difference is not always hierarchical. Sometimes, different is just different.

The purpose of this book is not to say good friends over everybody else, but to zoom into the puzzle piece of good friendship in particular—without framing it as the only model for human connection. It is critical, but not singular. How you assemble the remaining pieces depends on your box's distinct picture.

It is not good friends or no friends. The future is long, and you cannot yet imagine what any single relation will become to you, if you allow it the grace.

Afterword

I WANT TO share more about this book's origins; particularly, about the context in which I wrote it. After advocating for racial literacy with Winona, we separated into different colleges. By this time, I had experienced a friendship that I never saw or heard of before. Winona and I called each other "platonic life partners"; yet, we noticed our unusualness.

We were invited to speak in New York City sophomore year, but event organizers cautioned that they could only fit one chair onstage. Only room for one of you. Pick who. This happened regularly. In countless organizing spaces, speaking engagements, and national press, we noticed no friends are represented; everybody arrived as individuals. Thirteen emails later, however, event organizers conceded to allowing us both.

Winona took a train from Boston, where she was in

college, and we met in New Jersey, finishing homework in a car to New York City. Travel takes you from the familiar, but the act of traveling, especially with Winona, felt most familiar to me.

The event venue was a hotel with dark wood, high gothic ceilings, champagne glasses in the manicured hands of a mostly white audience, and—about thirty feet of stage. Somebody was saying something to me, something about dinner afterward, but his voice melted into the bordering bustle. Anger, thudding heat, rippled behind my eyelids. I looked at Winona, nodding my chin toward the stage.

Look. There was always space for two chairs.

Returning to campus, a question persisted: what is it about friendship? Why is it so hard to keep a good friend? It was through my independent research as an African American Studies major at Princeton University that I could pursue some answers.

At first, I was majoring in what was called the Woodrow Wilson School of Public and International Affairs. Spring semester, a guest lecturer, a political strategist and organizer, had paid a visit to my class. She asked what our majors were, and I replied unthinkingly, "Woody Woo." She pointed out that Woodrow Wilson, President of Princeton and later of the United States, prevented Black students from joining Princeton and supported the Ku Klux

Klan. Why study in his lineage, if his imagination was *so* limited that envisioning Black students (and thus, probably me too) as full human beings seemed to be a strain? Learning in Wilson's legacy would be like painting with one color, when much more expensive palettes existed.

I switched to African American Studies. It was not about choosing one department over the other, but about placing myself in one lineage over the other. Lineage means tradition, an intellectual genealogy you inherit from whomever you are learning from, and thus whoever they learned from, and whoever *they* learned from, and so on. If the lineage I was leaping from was a white-centric one, my thinking would flop. I wanted to climb higher, to the radical minds of intellectuals like Ida B. Wells and James Baldwin.

Whatever reductive idea you have about African American Studies, that it is only about African American people or "Black problems," is wrong. African American Studies labors to not only dent anti-Black racism, as if fixing only one tile in a broken roof, but seeks to repair the entire roof. Everyone stays dry because of African American Studies' contributions. Investing in African American Studies means investing in you, whoever you are. We all become better equipped to face racism and its interlocking systems of oppression, in order to think and resist our way toward freedom—not for one group, but for us all. This is why studying friendship in African American Studies' lineage made most sense to me.

While beginning this book for my senior thesis, I would walk through the campus's twirling red leaves, observing the gothic architecture that made the world feel crowded and self-important. I looked at students with knee-length boots, books in arms, scarves around their necks. I thought about my roommates, one who was born in Egypt but raised in Maryland, one born in New Jersey to Russian immigrants, and one born and raised in Lahore, Pakistan. In winter, walking through newly barren trees, I thought about the military uniform a classmate wore, the campus Imam who always said hi, and the director of Student Life, who often reminisced about her childhood in the Dominican Republic. We were like atoms, with different valences, repelling and attracting, twirling like those red leaves, thrumming with particular, ever so complicated political dynamics as we orbited one another.

How could I write about friendship, I wondered, in ways that reconciled this complexity? June Jordan became my answer. Here was someone who not only wrote beautifully about friendship, but who did so without skimming over its political intricacies.

You should know, there is a reason why you might not have known about June before reading this book. June often prioritized others' well-being over her own prestige, public recognition, wealth, and career. The *Washington Post* still said she was "a minor note," and "not famous enough to command a lot of attention," even after she had already authored nine books.[1] For June, publishing theory was not nearly as important as practicing it was with her friends.

"Publishers refused to work with her," June's student Sriram Shamasunder writes, pointing out the obvious gaps in her bibliography that align with times she advocated for those in Palestine and Nicaragua. She was too outspoken.

"This may in part be the reason she is not as widely read as her contemporaries like Alice Walker and Toni Morrison."[2]

I hope, then, that this book will motivate you to pick up some of June's work. Between her memoir, poetry, essays, and children's books, you could spend a lifetime dwelling inside her prolific writing.

I hope too that one day this book will exist alongside many others about friendship. Friendship is ever-changing, ever evolving. Any work about friendship is incomplete by itself. It must exist with others for a full picture.

Until then, consider this my contribution, completed with the support of my friends.

Acknowledgments

For my friends. Winona, you kick-started everything. Nastasia, so much of the joy in these pages comes from you. Thank you for your brilliance. Châu and Ariana, through some silly luck I met you both; thank you for getting me out of my head and into the city again. Johanne, my thought partner, I trusted your brain most with an early draft of this book. Thank you for your wonderful edits. Nora, thank you for your generous insights as well. Marina, Wafa, Marie Louise, Sophia, Betsy, and Nishat, even though you all were far, your friendships kept me company as I wrote.

Professors Eddie S. Glaude and Ruha Benjamin, you equipped me with the confidence needed to write. June Jordan's friend Alexis De Veaux told me she did not know she was smart until June told her, and you both did that for me. I am lucky to be your student. Jordan Skinner, thank you for your notes when this book was just an undergraduate thesis. John McPhee, you were the first person to call me a writer and that mattered more than you know.

Thank you also to my agent, Lynn Johnston. I feel so capable with you by my side. You believed in this book, saw what it could be, and pushed it toward that vision. Krishan Trotman, my publisher and editor, thank you for caring about every word, and for sticking with this project. Brea Baker, my other editor who swooped in and jogged alongside me to the finish line, your gentle nudges both exposed gaps in my thinking and somehow energized me to fill them. I am beyond grateful. Thank you also to Adrienne Torf for sharing stories about June over teas and dinner. Thank you to Pratibha Parmar, Alexis De Veaux, Kathy Engel, Ethelbert Miller, Mahito Indi Henderson, Amina Iro, and the rest of the Legacy Lit team too.

Last, thank you, Mom, Dad, Aaron, and Obi, who I miss dearly. You all made me believe I could write. And thank you to Kai, who curled up beside me through those long days as I wrote this.

Notes

INTRODUCTION: THE HABIT OF FRIENDSHIP

1 Eyer, "Translation from Plato's Republic 514b–518d ('Allegory of the Cave')."

2 Gendler, "Plato's Allegory of the Cave."

3 Cicero, *Laelius on Friendship*, section 22.

CHAPTER ONE: FRIENDSHIPS OF VIRTUE

1 Aristotle, *Nicomachean Ethics,* Book 8.

2 Hsu, *Stay True*, 21.

3 Aristotle, *Nicomachean Ethics,* Book 8.

4 Hsu, *Stay True*, 93.

5 Aristotle, *Nicomachean Ethics,* Book 8.

CHAPTER TWO: THE INDIVIDUAL

1 *Britannica*, "Henry David Thoreau—Transcendentalism, Walden Pond, Nature," accessed April 27, 2024. https://

www.britannica.com/biography/Henry-David-Thoreau
/Move-to-Walden-Pond.

2   Jordan, *Some of Us Did Not Die*, 109–19.

3   *American Masters*, "Toni Morrison: The Pieces I Am."

4   Ralph Waldo Emerson House, "The Home of Ralph Waldo
    Emerson: Emerson's Walks in Concord," accessed April
    27, 2024. https://www.ralphwaldoemersonhouse.org
    /emersons-walks-2.

5   Aristotle, *Nicomachean Ethics,* Book 8.

6   "Cartoons from the April 10, 2023, Issue." *New Yorker*,
    April 10, 2023. https://www.newyorker.com/gallery
    /cartoons-from-the-april-10-2023-issue.

7   Busch, "'Loneliness Epidemic' Hits Gen Z Hardest."

8   Aristotle, *Nicomachean Ethics,* Book 8.

9   Purtill and Tilley, "The Other Steve."

10 Boyle, *Steve Jobs*.

11 Beck and Rashid, "How to Talk to People."

12 Kleon, "Thoreau's Laundry."

13 Jordan, *Some of Us Did Not Die*, 89.

14 Jordan, 91.

15 Jordan, 116–19.

CHAPTER THREE: POLITICS OF FRIENDSHIP

1   Schweitzer, "Making Equals," 341.

2   Vesely, *Friendship and Virtue Ethics in the Book of Job*,
    50–52.

3   Strikwerda and May, "Male Friendship and Intimacy."

4   Margulies, "Frances Fox Piven."

5   Jordan, *Some of Us Did Not Die*, 257–67.

6   Walhof, "Friendship, Otherness, and Gadamer's Politics of Solidarity," 578.

7   Jordan, *Life as Activism*, 57.

8   Vesely, *Friendship and Virtue Ethics in the Book of Job*, 52.

9   Aristotle, *Nicomachean Ethics,* Book 8.

10 Schweitzer, "Making Equals," 345.

11 Tóibín, "The Unsparing Confessions of 'Giovanni's Room.'"

12 Baldwin, *The Price of the Ticket*, 443–47.

13 Hsu, "What Jacques Derrida Understood About Friendship."

14 Baldwin, *The Price of the Ticket*, 443–47.

15 Parker, *Movement in Black*, 68.

16 Amelia Montooth, Instagram post, April 1, 2024. https://www.instagram.com/reel/C5OU_TULYEQ/.

17 *American Heritage Dictionary* online, "friend," accessed May 2, 2024. https://ahdictionary.com/word/search.html?q=friend.

18 Schweitzer, "Making Equals," 341.

19 Schweitzer, 340.

20 Jordan, *Some of Us Did Not Die*, 153.

CHAPTER FOUR: FRIENDS MAKE THE WORLD BETTER

1   Mejías-Rentas, "How Angela Davis Ended Up on the FBI Most Wanted List."

2   Davis, "Tribute to June Jordan."

3   Parmar, *A Place of Rage*.

4   Jordan, *Some of Us Did Not Die*, 63–74.

5   Jordan, 88–89.

6   Aristotle, *Nicomachean Ethics,* Book 8.

7   Jordan, *Some of Us Did Not Die*, 219.

8   Davis, "Tribute to June Jordan."

9   "Black Writers in Praise of Toni Morrison," *New York Times*, advertisement, January 24, 1988, https://archive.nytimes.com/www.nytimes.com/books/98/01/11/home/15084.html?_r=2.

10   *American Masters*, "Toni Morrison: The Pieces I Am."

11   Kastor, "'Beloved' and the Protest."

12   Gold, "'Browder v. Gayle.'"

13   Zinn Education Project, "May 19, 1921."

14   Maranzani, "Yuri Kochiyama and Malcolm X's Boundary-Breaking Friendship."

15   Democracy Now!, "Yuri Kochiyama Remembers Malcolm X's Assassination & Living at WWII Japanese American Detention Camp."

16   Zinn Education Project, "May 19, 1921."

17   Garver, "The Rhetoric of Friendship in Plato's Lysis."

18   Mahdawi, "Black Lives Matter's Alicia Garza."

19   Martin Luther King, Jr. Research and Education Institute, "Abernathy, Ralph David."

20   Jordan, "Poem for South African Women."

CHAPTER FIVE: LAUGHING WITH FRIENDS

1 Freeman, "Fran Lebowitz."

2 *American Masters*, "Toni Morrison: Pieces I Am." https://www.pbs.org/video/fran-outtakes-2se2ol/.

3 Freeman, "Fran Lebowitz."

4 *American Masters*, "Toni Morrison: Pieces I Am." https://www.pbs.org/video/fran-outtakes-2se2ol/.

5 *Paris Review*, "Remembering Toni."

6 Strout, "What Is 'Type II Fun?'"

7 Gibran, "On Joy and Sorrow by Kahlil Gibran."

8 Cicero, *Laelius on Friendship*, section 22.

9 Jordan, *Life as Activism*, 14–16.

10 Brown, *Pleasure Activism*, 13.

11 Malaklou, "Loving with Bell, Leaping with Fanon, and Landing Nowhere," 68.

12 Pierce, "Ch. 2: The Boycott Begins."

13 Brown, *Pleasure Activism*, 1–20.

CHAPTER SIX: MAKING FRIENDS

1 Bhatia et al., "Study of Elite College Admissions Data Suggests Being Very Rich Is Its Own Qualification."

2 Claybourn, Cole. "How Much Is an Ivy Degree Worth?"

3 Miller et al., "Vast New Study Shows a Key to Reducing Poverty."

4 Ibid.

5 Kaplan, "If You Want to Get Rich, Make Rich Friends."

6   Ingraham, "Three Quarters of Whites Don't Have Any Non-White Friends."

7   Etymonline, "crony," accessed June 27, 2024, https://www.etymonline.com/word/crony.

8   Blee, *Women of the Klan*.

9   Jordan, *Life as Activism*, 9.

10 Hunt, *Fierce Tenderness*.

11 Jordan, *Life as Activism*, 126.

12 Jordan, *Some of Us Did Not Die*, 6.

CHAPTER SEVEN: BAD FRIENDSHIP

1   Emerson, "Friendship."

2   Murao, "Beat Generation Photos by Rob Lee."

3   Erickson and Jordan, "After Identity," 141.

4   *Britannica*, "Idi Amin," accessed March 3, 2024, https://www.britannica.com/biography/Idi-Amin.

5   Erickson and Jordan, "After Identity," 142.

6   Saliba, "June Jordan's Songs of Palestine and Lebanon."

7   Jordan, "Moving towards Home."

8   Jordan, *Some of Us Did Not Die*, 6.

9   Jordan, *Life as Activism*, 220.

10 Rich, *Feminist Postcolonial Theory*, "Notes Toward a Politics of Location," 1.2.

11 Erickson and Jordan, "After Identity," 142.

12 Rich, *Feminist Postcolonial Theory*, "Notes Toward a Politics of Location," 1.2.

13 Narula, "Additions, Subtractions."

14 Erickson and Jordan, "After Identity," 142.

15 Rich, "Blood, Bread and Poetry."

16 Doherty, "Remembering Adrienne Rich."

17 Aristotle, *Nicomachean Ethics,* Book 8.

CHAPTER EIGHT: FRIENDSHIP WITH MEN

1 Deresiewicz, "A Man. A Woman. Just Friends?"

2 Babcock et al., "Nice Girls Don't Ask."

3 Schumann and Ross, "Why Women Apologize More than Men."

4 Aristotle, *Nicomachean Ethics,* Book 8.

5 Ward, "Men and Women Can't Be 'Just Friends.'"

6 *1A,* "I Love You, Man."

7 Strikwerda and May, "Male Friendship and Intimacy."

CHAPTER NINE: LOVE

1 Perel, "Safety vs. Adventure in Relationships."

2 Mlambo-Ngcuka, "The Fantasy of the Nuclear Family Is Holding Us Back."

3 Federici, *Wages against Housework.*

4 Admin, "Black Families Severed by Slavery."

5 Mizielinska, "Is She Still a Family or Rather Some Stranger?"

6 Lewis, *Abolish the Family.*

7 Jordan, *On Call*, 19–26.

8 Cox, "The State of American Friendship."

9 Jaffe, *Work Won't Love You Back.*

10 Gumbs, "The Shape of My Impact."

11   Santas, "Plato's Theory of Eros in the Symposium."

12   Lorde, *Uses of the Erotic*.

13   Ferguson, "Blood Is Thicker Than Water."

14   hooks, *All about Love*, 134.

15   Bieber, "Revealing Divorce Statistics In 2024—Forbes Advisor."

CHAPTER TEN: FRIENDS LEARN TOGETHER

1   Harney and Moten, *The Undercommons*, 110.

2   Harney and Moten, *The Undercommons*.

3   May, *The Courage to Create*, 89.

4   Taylor, *How We Get Free*.

5   Ibid.

6   Narula, "Additions, Subtractions."

7   Frye, *Willful Virgin*.

8   Thorsson, *The Sisterhood*.

9   Democracy Now!, "'I Am a Renegade, an Outlaw, a Pagan.'"

10   Etymonline, "academy," accessed April 27, 2024. https://www.etymonline.com/word/academy.

11   McLaughlin, "Introduction to Philosophy."

12   Schweitzer, "Making Equals," 340.

13   *Daily Mail*, "Superbugs Could Be Destroyed with Sheeting Inspired by Shark Skin."

14   Harney and Moten, *The Undercommons*, 110.

CHAPTER ELEVEN: A FRIEND NAMED MENTOR

1 O'Donnell, "The Odyssey's Millennia-Old Model of Mentorship."

2 Andersen, "Cogeneration."

3 *Stanford Social Innovation Review* "Meeting the Multigenerational Moment."; Caron, "The Loneliness Curve."

4 Strott, "Intergenerational Friendship."

5 Ibid.

6 Child Crime Prevention & Safety Center, "Children and Grooming/Online Predators," accessed June 27, 2024. https://childsafety.losangelescriminallawyer.pro/children-and-grooming-online-predators.html.

7 Jordan, *Some of Us Did Not Die*, 294.

8 Schwartz, "When June Jordan and Buckminster Fuller Tried to Redesign Harlem."

9 Jordan, *Some of Us Did Not Die*, 294.

10 Buckminster Fuller Institute, "Biography."

11 Poetry Foundation, "R. Buckminster Fuller"; Tomkins, "Buckminster Fuller, Intellectual Outlaw."

12 "Interview with E. D. Nixon."

13 Pigliucci, *Answers for Aristotle*.

14 Rankin, "And Still She Rises."

15 Charney, "Maya Angelou."

16 Chambers, "Published More Than 50 Years Ago, 'I Know Why the Caged Bird Sings' Launched a Revolution."

17 Martin Luther King, Jr. Research and Education Institute, "Angelou, Maya."

18 Morrison, "James Baldwin: His Voice Remembered."

19   Democracy Now!, "On This Juneteenth."

20   Halliday, "Witness Maya Angelou & James Baldwin's
     Close Friendship."

21   Goodings, "My Hero."

CHAPTER TWELVE: THE UNREMITTING FRIEND

1   Malaklou, "Loving with Bell, Leaping with Fanon, and
     Landing Nowhere," 67–68.

2   Deng, "Here's What bell hooks' Friends and Colleagues
     Want You to Remember about Her."

3   Fairchild, *The Blue Buick*, 31.

4   Malaklou, "Loving with Bell, Leaping with Fanon, and
     Landing Nowhere." 68, Deng, "'Unapologetic in the Priori-
     tization of Black Women.'"

5   Berea College, "Get to Know bell hooks."

6   Malaklou, "Loving with Bell, Leaping with Fanon, and
     Landing Nowhere," 69.

7   hooks, *All about Love*, 45.

8   Jordan, *Some of Us Did Not Die*, 47–51.

9   Baldwin, *The Price of the Ticket*, 443–47.

10   Rich, *On Lies, Secrets, and Silence*, 234.

11   Jordan, *Some of Us Did Not Die*, 261.

12   hooks, *All about Love*, 34.

13   hooks, *All about Love, 45*.

14   Jordan, *Some of Us Did Not Die*, 258.

15   Quirk, "The Harsh Truth About Brutal Honesty.

16   Ibid.

17   Abramovitch, "Tom Holland Breaks Free."

CHAPTER THIRTEEN: FRIENDS FAR AWAY

1   Friends, "The Secret Meaning of Keep in Touch."

2   "You Can Only Rely on 4 of Your 150 Facebook Friends—
    Here's Why That's Not so Bad."

3   "Learn Public Speaking from Cicero, the Roman Senator
    Who Defied Julius Caesar."

4   Sullivan, "From 'Sister Love.'"

5   Cicero, *Letters to Atticus*, CCXCVII (A VII, 7).

6   Cicero, *Letters to Atticus*, CCLXVII (A VI, 4).

7   Aristotle, *Nicomachean Ethics*, Book 8.

8   Enszer, ed., *Sister Love*, 57.

9   Cicero, *Letters to Atticus*, IV (A I, 9).

10 Cicero, *Letters to Atticus*, CCXCVI (A VII, 6).

11 Cicero, *Letters to Atticus*, CCXCVII (A VII, 7).

12 Cicero, *Letters to Atticus*, CCCII (A VII, 10).

13 Enszer, ed., *Sister Love*, 78.

14 Enszer, ed., *Sister Love*, 44.

15 Cicero, *Letters*, Year v4 44.

16 Cicero, *Letters to Atticus*, "Perseus Under Philologic,"
    1.18.6.

17 Enszer, ed., *Sister Love*, 112–113.

CHAPTER FOURTEEN: GOODBYE, FRIEND

1   Brandolini, "My TikTok On Friendship Breakups Went
    Viral."

2   Ibid.

3 Marías, "Javier Marías on the Pain of Drifting Apart from Old Friends."

4 Margulies, "Frances Fox Piven."

5 Whyte, *Consolations*, 83.

6 Jordan, *Some of Us Did Not Die*, 266–67.

7 Jones, "'If Black Women Were Free.'"

8 Pilat, "The Sunk Cost Fallacy."

9 Popova, "Steinbeck and the Difficult Art of the Friend Breakup."

10 Ibid.

11 McCoy, "Friendship and Moral Failure in Aristotle's Ethics."

CHAPTER FIFTEEN: BOUNDARIES

1 Schweitzer, "Making Equals," 342–345.

2 D'Astice and Russell, "Enmeshment in Couples and Families."

3 Schweitzer, "Making Equals," 348.

4 Chirkov, "Culture, Personal Autonomy and Individualism."

5 Human Rights Campaign Foundation, "Attacks on Gender Affirming Care by State Map."

6 Bennice, "Marital Rape."

7 Govier, "Self-Trust, Autonomy, and Self-Esteem."

8 Jordan, "Moving towards Home."

9 Tanna, "Brene Brown."

10 Halliday, "Witness Maya Angelou & James Baldwin's Close Friendship."

11 Taylor, "Beyond 'Obligatory Camaraderie.'"

CHAPTER SIXTEEN: JUST FRIENDS

1   Ramsey and Ogden, *Tractatus Logico-Philosophicus*.

AFTERWORD

1   De Witt, "June Jordan."

2   Shamasunder, "June Jordan's Legacy of Solidarity & Love."

Bibliography

Abramovitch, Seth. "Tom Holland Breaks Free: Talking Zendaya, 'The Crowded Room' and the Future of Spider-Man." *Hollywood Reporter* (blog), June 14, 2023. https://www.hollywoodreporter.com/feature/tom-holland-the-crowded-room-future-spider-man-1235514347/.

Admin, Madeo. "Black Families Severed by Slavery." Equal Justice Initiative, January 29, 2018, https://eji.org/news/history-racial-injustice-black-families-severed-by-slavery/.

Aristotle. *Nicomachean Ethics*. Internet Classics Archive, accessed April 27, 2024. https://classics.mit.edu/Aristotle/nicomachaen.html.

Babcock, Linda, Sara Laschever, Michele Gelfand, and Deborah Small. "Nice Girls Don't Ask." *Harvard Business Review*, October 1, 2003. https://hbr.org/2003/10/nice-girls-dont-ask.

Baldwin, James. *The Price of the Ticket: Collected Nonfiction, 1948–1985*, 443–47. New York: St. Martin's Press, 1985. https://www.scribd.com/doc/97323735/Baldwin-James-Sweet-Lorraine.

Beck, Julie, and Rebecca Rashid, hosts, "How to Not Go It Alone," *How to Talk to People* (podcast), July 20, 2023. https://www.youtube.com/watch?v=6_0MjAUAVJQ.

Bennice, Jennifer A. and Patricia A. Resick. "Marital Rape: History, Research, and Practice." *Trauma, Violence, & Abuse* 4, no. 3 (July 2003). https://www.ojp.gov/ncjrs/virtual-library/abstracts/marital-rape-history-research-and-practice.

Berea College. "Get to Know bell hooks." Accessed May 9, 2024. https://www.berea.edu/centers/the-bell-hooks-center/about-bell/.

Bhatia, Aatish, Claire Cain Miller, and Josh Katz. "Study of Elite College Admissions Data Suggests Being Very Rich Is Its Own Qualification." *New York Times*, July 24, 2023. https://www.nytimes.com/interactive/2023/07/24/upshot/ivy-league-elite-college-admissions.html.

Bieber, Christy. "Revealing Divorce Statistics in 2024." *Forbes Advisor*, May 30, 2024. https://www.forbes.com/advisor/legal/divorce/divorce-statistics/.

Blee, Kathleen M. *Women of the Klan: Racism and Gender in the 1920s.* Berkeley: University of California Press, 2009.

Boyle, Danny, dir. *Steve Jobs.* Universal Pictures, 2015.

Brandolini, Dr. Arianna. "My TikTok on Friendship Breakups Went Viral. Here's What We Can All Learn." *Forbes.* March 3, 2023. https://www.forbes.com/sites/drariannabrandolini/2023/03/03/my-tiktok-on-friendship-breakups-went-viral-heres-what-we-can-all-learn/.

Brinkhof, Tim. "Learn Public Speaking from Cicero, the Roman Senator Who Defied Julius Caesar," Big Think. November 3, 2022. https://bigthink.com/the-past/cicero-public-speaking/.

Brown, Adrienne Maree. *Pleasure Activism: The Politics of Feeling Good*. Edinburgh: AK Press, 2019.

Buckminster Fuller Institute. "Biography." Accessed December 7, 2021. https://www.bfi.org/about-fuller/biography/.

Busch, Jason. "'Loneliness Epidemic' Hits Gen Z Hardest: 1 in 4 Are Lonely at Work." *In Business*, July 29, 2021. https://www.ibmadison.com/industries/employment-hr/loneliness-epidemic-hits-gen-z-hardest-1-in-4-are-lonely-at-work/article_2c72b43e-6b07-5aa0-b10e-8e20d21abba9.html.

Call Your Friends. "The Secret Meaning of Keep in Touch." Accessed May 9, 2024. https://callyourfriends.io/keep-in-touch/.

Caron, Christina. "The Loneliness Curve." *New York Times*, May 6, 2024. https://www.nytimes.com/2024/05/06/well/loneliness-mental-health-age.html.

Chambers, Veronica. "Published More Than 50 Years Ago, 'I Know Why the Caged Bird Sings' Launched a Revolution." *Smithsonian*, January 2020. https://www.smithsonianmag.com/arts-culture/published-50-years-ago-i-know-why-caged-bird-sings-launched-revolution-180973719/.

Charney, Noah. "Maya Angelou: How I Write." *Daily Beast*, April 10, 2013. https://www.thedailybeast.com/articles/2013/04/10/maya-angelou-how-i-write.

Chirkov, Valery. "Culture, Personal Autonomy and Individualism: Their Relationships and Implications for Personal Growth and Well-Being." In *Perspectives and Progress in Contemporary Cross-Cultural Psychology*. International Association for Cross-Cultural Psychology, 2008. https://doi.org/10.4087/IFQE7624.

Cicero, Marcus Tullius. *Laelius on Friendship*, section 22. Perseus Digital Library, accessed May 1, 2024. https://www.perseus.tufts.edu/hopper/text?doc=Cic.%20Amic.%2022.82&lang=original.

Cicero, Marcus Tullius. *Letters*, v4 44. Perseus Digital Library, accessed May 9, 2024. https://www.perseus.tufts.edu/hopper/text?doc=Perseus%3Atext%3A1999.02.0022%3Ayear%3Dv4%2044&force=y.

Cicero, Marcus Tullius. *Letters to Atticus*. Perseus Digital Library, accessed May 9, 2024. https://www.perseus.tufts.edu/hopper/text?doc=Perseus%3Atext%3A1999.02.0022%3Atext%3DA%3Abook%3D7%3Aletter%3D10.

Claybourn, Cole. "How Much Is an Ivy Degree Worth?" *U.S. News*. Jan 30, 2023. https://www.usnews.com/education/best-colleges/articles/how-much-is-an-ivy-league-degree-worth.

Cox, Daniel A. "The State of American Friendship: Change, Challenges, and Loss." Survey Center on American Life, June 8, 2021. https://www.americansurveycenter.org/research/the-state-of-american-friendship-change-challenges-and-loss/.

Daily Mail. "Superbugs Could Be Destroyed with Sheeting Inspired by Shark Skin." June 14, 2018. http://www.dailymail.co.uk/health/article-5841913/Hospital-superbugs-destroyed-sheeting-inspired-shark-skin.html.

D'Astice, Teresa, and William P. Russell. "Enmeshment in Couples and Families." In *Encyclopedia of Couple and Family Therapy*, edited by Jay L. Lebow, Anthony L. Chambers, and Douglas C. Breunlin, 911–15. Springer Cham, Switzerland, 2019. https://doi.org/10.1007/978-3-319-49425-8_1021.

Davis, Angela. "Tribute to June Jordan." *Meridians* 3, no. 2 (2003): 1–2.

Democracy Now! "'I Am a Renegade, an Outlaw, a Pagan': Author, Poet and Activist Alice Walker in Her Own Words." February 13, 2006. http://www.democracynow.org/2006/2/13/i_am_a_renegade_an_outlaw.

Democracy Now! "On This Juneteenth, the Oldest Known Celebration of the End of Slavery, We Celebrate the Legacy of Activist and Poet June Jordan." June 19, 2002. http://www.democracynow.org/2002/6/19/on_this_juneteenth_the_oldest_known.

Democracy Now! "Yuri Kochiyama Remembers Malcolm X's Assassination & Living at WWII Japanese American Detention Camp." Accessed May 2, 2024. http://www.democracynow.org/2006/2/21/civil_rights_activist_yuri_kochiyama_remembers.

Deng, Jireh. "Here's What bell hooks' Friends and Colleagues Want You to Remember about Her." NPR, February 5, 2022. https://www.bpr.org/post/heres-what-bell-hooks-friends-and-colleagues-want-you-remember-about-her#stream%2f0.

Deng, Jireh. "'Unapologetic in the Prioritization of Black Women': bell hooks Remembered by Loved Ones." KQED, December 29, 2021. https://www.kqed.org/news/11900423/unapologetic-in-the-prioritization-of-black-women-bell-hooks-remembered-by-loved-ones.

Deresiewicz, William. "A Man. A Woman. Just Friends?" *New York Times*, April 7, 2012. https://www.nytimes.com/2012/04/08/opinion/sunday/a-man-a-woman-just-friends.html.

De Witt, Karen. "June Jordan: On the Brink of Fame." *Washington Post*, October 12, 1977. https://www.washingtonpost.com/archive/lifestyle/1977/10/13/june-jordan-on-the-brink-of-fame/f56ffe43-ffbf-4219-a2cd-88076f4ecfe9/.

Doherty, Benjamin. "Remembering Adrienne Rich: Poet, Activist and Supporter of Palestinian Liberation." Electronic Intifada, March 29, 2012. https://electronicintifada.net/blogs /benjamin-doherty/remembering-adrienne-rich-poet-activist -and-supporter-palestinian-liberation.

Emerson, Ralph Waldo. "Friendship." *Essays*. Accessed April 27, 2024, https://archive.vcu.edu/english/engweb/transcendentalism /authors/emerson/essays/friendship.html.

Enszer, Julie, ed. *Sister Love: The Letters of Audre Lorde and Pat Parker 1974–1989*. New York: A Midsummer Night's Press, 2018.

Erickson, Peter, and June Jordan. "After Identity." *Transition*, no. 63 (1994): 132–49. https://doi.org/10.2307/2935338.

Eyer, Shawn. "Translation from Plato's Republic 514b–518d ('Allegory of the Cave')." *Ahiman: A Review of Masonic Culture and Tradition* 1 (2009): 73–78.

Fairchild, B. H. *The Blue Buick: New and Selected Poems*. New York: W. W. Norton, 2014.

Federici, Silvia. *Wages against Housework*. Bristol, UK: Falling Wall Press, 1975.

Ferguson, Ashleigh. "Blood Is Thicker Than Water: Definition, Meaning, Origin, and Examples." ProWritingAid. Accessed June 28, 2024. https://prowritingaid.com/blood-is-thicker -than-water.

Freedman, Marc, and Eunice Lin Nichols. "Cogeneration." CoGenerate, accessed June 27, 2024. https://cogenerate.org /research/cogeneration/.

Freeman, Hadley. "Fran Lebowitz: 'If People Disagree with Me, So What?'" *Guardian*, August 28, 2021. https://www.theguardian.com/books/2021/aug/28/fran-lebowitz-if-people-disagree-with-me-so-what.

Frye, Marilyn. *Willful Virgin: Essays in Feminism, 1976–1992.* Freedom, CA: Crossing Press, 1992.

Garver, Eugene. "The Rhetoric of Friendship in Plato's Lysis." *Rhetorica: A Journal of the History of Rhetoric* 24, no. 2 (2006): 127–46, https://doi.org/10.1525/rh.2006.24.2.127.

Gendler, Alex. "Plato's Allegory of the Cave." YouTube, 2015. https://www.youtube.com/watch?v=1RWOpQXTltA.

Gibran, Kahlil. "On Joy and Sorrow." Poets.org, accessed May 3, 2024. https://poets.org/poem/joy-and-sorrow.

Gold, Jonathan. "'Browder v. Gayle.'" SPLC Learning for Justice, April 29, 2016. https://www.learningforjustice.org/magazine/summer-2016/browder-v-gayle.

Goodings, Lennie. "My Hero: Maya Angelou by Her Publisher Lennie Goodings." *Guardian*, May 29, 2014, https://www.theguardian.com/books/2014/may/29/my-hero-maya-angelou-by-lennie-goodings.

Govier, Trudy. "Self-Trust, Autonomy, and Self-Esteem." *Hypatia* 8, no. 1 (1993): 99–120.

Greenfield-Sanders, Timothy, dir. *American Masters.* Season 34, episode 3, "Toni Morrison: The Pieces I Am." Aired June 1, 2020, on PBS.

Gumbs, Alexis Pauline. "The Shape of My Impact." Feminist Wire, October 29, 2012. https://thefeministwire.com/2012/10/the-shape-of-my-impact/.

Halliday, Ayun. "Witness Maya Angelou & James Baldwin's Close Friendship in a TV Interview from 1975." Open Culture, October 11, 2021. https://www.openculture.com/2021/10/witness-maya-angelou-james-baldwins-close-friendship-in-a-tv-interview-from-1975.html.

Harney, Stefano, and Fred Moten. *The Undercommons: Fugitive Planning & Black Study.* Wivenhoe, UK: Minor Compositions, 2013.

hooks, bell. *All about Love: New Visions.* New York: William Morrow, 2018.

Hsu, Hua. *Stay True: A Memoir.* New York: Doubleday, 2022.

Hsu, Hua. "What Jacques Derrida Understood About Friendship." *New Yorker*, December 3, 2019. https://www.newyorker.com/books/second-read/what-jacques-derrida-understood-about-friendship.

Human Rights Campaign Foundation. "Attacks on Gender Affirming Care by State Map." Accessed May 7, 2024. https://www.hrc.org/resources/attacks-on-gender-affirming-care-by-state-map.

Hunt, Mary E. *Fierce Tenderness: A Feminist Theology of Friendship.* New York: Crossroad, 1991.

IA. "I Love You, Man: The Male Friendship Recession." June 8, 2023. https://www.npr.org/2023/06/08/1181170335/i-love-you-man-the-male-friendship-recession.

Ingraham, Christopher. "Three Quarters of Whites Don't Have Any Non-White Friends." *Washington Post*, November 25, 2021. https://www.washingtonpost.com/news/wonk/wp/2014/08/25/three-quarters-of-whites-dont-have-any-non-white-friends/.

Jaffe, Sarah. *Work Won't Love You Back: How Devotion to Our Jobs Keeps Us Exploited, Exhausted, and Alone.* New York: Bold Type Books, 2021.

Johnson, Henry, "Interview with E. D. Nixon." Washington University in St. Louis, Blackside Inc., February 23, 1979. Accessed May 7, 2024. http://repository.wustl.edu/concern /videos/v405sc21t.

Jones, Marian. "'If Black Women Were Free': An Oral History of the Combahee River Collective." *Nation*, October 29, 2021. https://www.thenation.com/article/society/combahee-river -collective-oral-history/.

Jordan, June. "Moving towards Home." Poetry Foundation, accessed April 27, 2024. https://www.poetryfoundation.org /poetrymagazine/poems/161355/moving-towards-home.

Jordan, June. *Life as Activism: June Jordan's Writings from the Progressive.* Sacramento, CA: Litwin Books, 2014.

Jordan, June. *On Call: Political Essays.* Boston: South End Press, 1985.

Jordan, June. "Poem for South African Women." Poets.org, accessed May 2, 2024. https://poets.org/poem/poem-south -african-women.

Jordan, June. *Some of Us Did Not Die: New and Selected Essays of June Jordan.* New York: Basic/Civitas Books, 2002.

Kaplan, Juliana. "If You Want to Get Rich, Make Rich Friends, a Harvard Economist Found in 2 New Studies." *Business Insider*, August 2, 2022. https://www.businessinsider.com/want-to-get -rich-make-rich-friends-harvard-reserach-study-2022-8.

Kastor, Elizabeth. "'Beloved' and the Protest." *Washington Post*, January 20, 1988. https://www.washingtonpost.com/archive /lifestyle/1988/01/21/beloved-and-the-protest/8bc8cb27-5607 -4cad-a3e1-26a0b20e0608/.

Kleon, Austin. "Thoreau's Laundry," Austin Kleon (blog), August 30, 2019. https://austinkleon.com/2019/08/30/thoreaus -laundry/.

Lewis, Sophie. *Abolish the Family: A Manifesto for Care and Liberation*. London: Verso, 2022.

Lippe, McGraw, Jordi. "Social Media Study Reveals You Can Only Count on 4 of Your 150 Facebook Friends." Today.com. February 1, 2016. https://www.today.com/health/social-media -study-reveals-you-can-only-count-4-your-t70316.

Lorde, Audre. *Uses of the Erotic: The Erotic as Power*. Freedom, CA: Crossing Press, 1978.

Mahdawi, Arwa. "Black Lives Matter's Alicia Garza: 'Leadership Today Doesn't Look like Martin Luther King.'" *Guardian*, October 17, 2020. https://www.theguardian.com/world/2020 /oct/17/black-lives-matter-alicia-garza-leadership-today -doesnt-look-like-martin-luther-king.

Malaklou, M. Shadee. "Loving with Bell, Leaping with Fanon, and Landing Nowhere." *Journal of French and Francophone Philosophy* 30, no. 2 (January 13, 2023): 66–77. https://doi .org/10.5195/jffp.2022.1022.

Maranzani, Barbara. "Yuri Kochiyama and Malcolm X's Boundary-Breaking Friendship," Biography.com, May 14, 2021. https://www.biography.com/activists/yuri-kochiyama -malcolm-x-friendship.

Maranzani, Barbara. "Yuri Kochiyama and Malcolm X's Boundary-Breaking Friendship," Biography. May 14, 2021. https://www.biography.com/activists/yuri-kochiyama -malcolm-x-friendship.

Margulies, Abby. "Frances Fox Piven: The Weight of the Poor." *Guernica*, September 15, 2011. https://www.guernicamag.com /west_piven_interview_9_15_11/.

Marías, Javier. "Javier Marías on the Pain of Drifting Apart from Old Friends." *Literary Hub* (blog), August 30, 2018. https://lithub.com/javier-marias-on-the-pain-of-drifting -apart-from-old-friends/.

Martin Luther King, Jr. Research and Education Institute. "Abernathy, Ralph David." Accessed May 2, 2024. https://king institute.stanford.edu/abernathy-ralph-david.

Martin Luther King, Jr. Research and Education Institute. "Angelou, Maya." Accessed May 7, 2024. https://kinginstitute .stanford.edu/angelou-maya.

May, Rollo. *The Courage to Create*. New York: Norton, 1975.

McCoy, Marina Berzins. *Wounded Heroes: Vulnerability as a Virtue in Ancient Greek Literature and Philosophy*. Oxford University Press, 2013. https://doi.org/10.1093/acprof :oso/9780199672783.003.0006.

McLaughlin, Jeff. "Introduction to Philosophy," Louis Pressbooks, January 1, 2024. https://louis.pressbooks.pub/introphilosophy /chapter/introduction-to-philosophy/.

Mejías-Rentas, Antonio. "How Angela Davis Ended Up on the FBI Most Wanted List," History. January 3, 2024, https:// www.history.com/news/angela-davis-fbi-most-wanted-list.

Miller, Claire Cain, Josh Katz, Francesca Paris, and Aatish Bhatia. "Vast New Study Shows a Key to Reducing Poverty: More Friendships Between Rich and Poor." *New York Times*, August 1, 2022. https://www.nytimes.com/interactive/2022/08/01/upshot/rich-poor-friendships.html.

Mizielińska, Joanna. "'Is She Still a Family or Rather Some Stranger?': Relative Strangers and Kinship Plasticity in Families of Choice in Poland." *Journal of Homosexuality* 68, no. 11 (September 19, 2021): 1899–1922. https://doi.org/10.1080/00918369.2020.1712143.

Mlambo-Ngcuka, Phumzile. "The Fantasy of the Nuclear Family Is Holding Us Back." CNN, August 8, 2019. https://www.cnn.com/2019/08/08/opinions/nuclear-family-revised-law-policy-mlambo-ngcuka/index.html.

Morrison, Toni. "James Baldwin: His Voice Remembered; Life in His Language." *New York Times*, December 20, 1987. https://archive.nytimes.com/www.nytimes.com/books/98/03/29/specials/baldwin-morrison.html?hc_location=ufi.

Murao, Shig. "Beat Generation Photos by Rob Lee." Empty Mirror, March 7, 2012. https://www.emptymirrorbooks.com/beat/lee.

O'Donnell, B. R. J. "The Odyssey's Millennia-Old Model of Mentorship." *Atlantic*, October 13, 2017. https://www.theatlantic.com/business/archive/2017/10/the-odyssey-mentorship/542676/.

Paris Review. "Remembering Toni." August 6, 2019. https://www.theparisreview.org/blog/2019/08/06/remembering-toni/.

Parker, Pat, *Movement in Black*. Ithaca, NY: Firebrand Books, 1999.

Parmar, Pratibha, dir. *A Place of Rage*, 1991.

Perel, Esther. "Safety vs. Adventure in Relationships." *Medium* (blog), November 10, 2014. https://medium.com/@EstherPerel /safety-vs-adventure-in-relationships-188b1292bb3a.

Pigliucci, Massimo. *Answers for Aristotle: How Science and Philosophy Can Lead Us to a More Meaningful Life.* New York: Basic Books, 2012.

Pilat, Dan and Dr. Sekoul Krastev. "The Sunk Cost Fallacy." The Decision Lab, accessed May 9, 2024. https://thedecisionlab .com/biases/the-sunk-cost-fallacy.

Poetry Foundation. "R. Buckminster Fuller." Accessed May 7, 2024. https://www.poetryfoundation.org/. https://www.poetry foundation.org/poets/r-buckminster-fuller.

Popova, Maria. "Steinbeck and the Difficult Art of the Friend Breakup." *The Marginalian* (blog), March 18, 2016. https:// www.themarginalian.org/2016/03/18/john-steinbeck-george -albee-friend-breakup-letter/.

Purtill, James and Tom Tilley. "The Other Steve: What Does Wozniak Really Think of Steve Jobs?," Triple J, August 23, 2016. https://www.abc.net.au/triplej/programs/hack/what -does-wozniak-really-think-of-steve-jobs/7777788.

Quirk, Michelle. "The Harsh Truth About Brutal Honesty." *Psychology Today*, January 24, 2023. https://www.psychology today.com/us/blog/childhood-emotional-neglect/202211 /beware-brutal-honesty-it-may-be-sign-toxic-person.

Ramsey, F. P., trans. and C. K. Ogden, ed. *Tractatus Logico- Philosophicus.* Ludwig Wittgenstein Project, accessed June 29, 2024. https://www.wittgensteinproject.org/w/index.php? title=Tractatus_Logico-Philosophicus_(English).

Rankin, Seji. "And Still She Rises: The EW Guide to Maya Angelou." *Entertainment Weekly*. September 20, 2020, https://ew.com/books/2020/01/20/maya-angelou-guide/.

Raqs Media Collective. "Additions, Subtractions: On Collectives and Collectivities," accessed on January 3, 2023. https://criticalcollective.in/ArtistGInner2.aspx?Aid=143&Eid=281.

Rich, Adrienne. *Feminist Postcolonial Theory*. Edinburgh University Press, 2003. https://doi.org/10.1515/9781474470254-004.

Rich, Adrienne. "Blood, Bread and Poetry: The Location of the Poet." *Massachusetts Review* 24, no. 3 (1983): 521–40.

Rich, Adrienne. *On Lies, Secrets, and Silence: Selected Prose 1966–1978*. New York: Norton, 1979.

Robinson, Jo Ann. *The Montgomery Bus Boycott and the Women Who Started It*, "Ch. 2: The Boycott Begins." Knoxville: University of Tennessee Press, May 22, 1987.

Saliba, Therese. "June Jordan's Songs of Palestine and Lebanon." Feminist Wire, March 24 2016. https://thefeministwire.com/2016/03/june-jordans-songs-of-palestine/.

Santas, Gerasimos. "Plato's Theory of Eros in the Symposium Abstract." *Noûs* 13, no. 1 (1979): 67–75. https://doi.org/10.2307/2214796.

Schumann, Karina, and Michael Ross. "Why Women Apologize More than Men: Gender Differences in Thresholds for Perceiving Offensive Behavior." *Psychological Science* 21, no. 11 (November 2010): 1649–55. https://doi.org/10.1177/0956797610384150.

Schwartz, Claire. "When June Jordan and Buckminster Fuller Tried to Redesign Harlem." *New Yorker*, August 22, 2020. https://www.newyorker.com/culture/culture-desk/when-june-jordan-and-buckminster-fuller-tried-to-redesign-harlem.

Schweitzer, Ivy. "Making Equals: Classical Philia and Women's Friendship." *Feminist Studies* 42, no. 2 (2016): 337–64. https://doi.org/10.15767/feministstudies.42.2.0337.

Shamasunder, Sriram. "June Jordan's Legacy of Solidarity & Love." DailyGood, February 14, 2023. https://www.dailygood.org/story/3044/june-jordan-s-legacy-of-solidarity-and-love-sriram-shamasunder/.

Stanford Social Innovation Review. "Meeting the Multigenerational Moment." Accessed June 27, 2024. https://ssir.org/meeting_the_multigenerational_moment.

Strikwerda, Robert A., and Larry May. "Male Friendship and Intimacy." *Hypatia* 7, no. 3 (1992): 110–25.

Strott, Steve. "Intergenerational Friendship." Denver Institute for Faith & Work, November 9, 2015. https://www.denverinstitute.org/intergenerational-friendship/.

Strout, Erin. "What Is 'Type II Fun,' and Why Do Some People Want to Have It?" *Washington Post*, March 24, 2022. https://www.washingtonpost.com/wellness/2022/03/24/what-is-type-2-fun/.

Sullivan, Mecca Jamilah. "From 'Sister Love: The Letters of Audre Lorde and Pat Parker.'" Public Books (blog), February 27, 2018. https://www.publicbooks.org/sister-love-letters-audre-lorde-pat-parker/.

Tanna. "Brene Brown: Boundaries, Empathy, and Compassion." *Mandarin Duck* (blog), January 31, 2017. https://annajwatson .wordpress.com/2017/01/31/brene-brown-boundaries -empathy-and-compassion/.

Taylor, Judith. "Beyond 'Obligatory Camaraderie': Girls' Friendship in Zadie Smith's NW and Jillian and Mariko Tamaki's Skim." *Feminist Studies* 42, no. 2 (2016): 445–68. https://doi .org/10.15767/feministstudies.42.2.0445.

Taylor, Keeanga-Yamahtta, ed. *How We Get Free: Black Feminism and the Combahee River Collective.* Chicago: Haymarket Books, 2017.

Thorsson, Courtney. *The Sisterhood: How a Network of Black Women Writers Changed American Culture.* New York: Columbia University Press, 2023.

Tóibín, Colm. "The Unsparing Confessions of 'Giovanni's Room.'" *New Yorker*, February 26, 2016. https://www.new yorker.com/books/page-turner/the-unsparing-confessions -of-giovannis-room.

Tomkins, Calvin. "Buckminster Fuller, Intellectual Outlaw." *New Yorker*, December 31, 1965. https://www.newyorker.com /magazine/1966/01/08/in-the-outlaw-area.

Vesely, Patricia. *Friendship and Virtue Ethics in the Book of Job.* Cambridge University Press, 2019.

Walhof, Darren R. "Friendship, Otherness, and Gadamer's Politics of Solidarity." *Political Theory* 34, no. 5 (October 2006): 569–93. https://doi.org/10.1177/0090591706290515.

Ward, Adrian F. "Men and Women Can't Be 'Just Friends.'" *Scientific American.* October 23, 2012. https://www.scientificamerican .com/article/men-and-women-cant-be-just-friends/.

Whyte, David. *Consolations: The Solace, Nourishment and Underlying Meaning of Everyday Words.* Langley, Washington: Many Rivers Press, 2014.

Zinn Education Project. "May 19, 1921: Yuri Kochiyama Born," accessed May 2, 2024. https://www.zinnedproject.org/news /tdih/yuri-kochiyama-was-born/.